THEY STILL SPEAK

Motivating Messages by Great Missionaries

Compiled by Rev. Howard L. Cummings

Library of Congress Card Number: 2006938445

ISBN 978-0-9790403-0-6

First Ministries
P. O. Box 440267
Aurora, CO 80044-0267

Printed in the U.S.A. by
Morris Publishing
3212 East Highway 30
Kearney, NE 68847
1-800-650-7888

Acknowledgments

I want to thank Margie, my lovely wife of over fifty years, who has stood beside me through the years of pastoring and traveled the globe in support of my missions passion.

Thanks as well to my secretary, Lois Crouch, for the countless hours of research and work on the manuscript.

I owe a debt of gratitude to each of the families of these missionary heroes who have not only granted permission to publish their loved one's sermon, but have offered encouragement and assistance in so many ways — the spelling of strange, foreign words, providing history of their ministry and biographic details in completing this work.

Cover design and illustration by Mike Bennett Graphics
www.mikebennettgraphics.com

TABLE OF CONTENTS

INTRODUCTION

THEY STILL SPEAK!

For almost 28 years, I was privileged to serve as Senior Pastor of what was then one of America's premier missions churches. Aurora First Assembly consistently gave unusually large amounts to support missionaries and missions projects around the globe. But, it was more than the proverbial "bottom line" on the annual report; the congregation was wholly committed to activities and attitudes which insured that succeeding generations would be sensitive to the Great Commission. Children's ministries featured a heartbeat for missions, youth activities were geared to global vision, including local and worldwide involvement, and adults were more than spectators — they led the way. Our annual missions crusade was the spiritual highlight of the church year with over a month of inspiring moments. And, throughout the years, some of the greatest career missionaries of this generation graced our pulpit.

It has occurred to me that, in addition to continuing my personal involvement in the missions enterprise, I can provide a real service to believers around the globe by sharing the messages some of these great missionaries gave us. Those in this volume feature messages by dedicated harvest hands who have now been received into the presence of the Lord of the harvest, whose parting words to the church became their first priority. These men were my friends — men I hunted with, traveled with, shared ministry with, and, with one, was honored to serve on his board. It is my sincere prayer that you are both blessed and motivated by their passion. They still speak!

"...he being dead yet speaks!"

— Hebrews 11:4

Howard Cummings, President
GLOBAL MANDATE

COMMENTS

"As a young pastor dreaming of building a great missions church, it didn't take me long to hear of the names and missions passions of Margie and Howard Cummings. Before they ever came to preach a Missions Convention for me, I was preaching some of Howard's missions sermons...and praying he wouldn't preach the same ones when he came to our church! The first convention he preached for me, our church doubled our Faith Promise giving and our missions journey had begun. Beginning with about $15,000 annually in our missions giving our first year in the pastorate, we were blessed to see our small church of about 375 people give over $400,000 to missions 12 years later when we left to become District Superintendent. Howard's great sermons were tools that helped me light the way for the people I loved! May this book of great missions messages, which motivated the author as his moved many of us, inspire a whole new generation of believers committed to the global mandate."

Rev. Joseph S. Girdler, Superintendent
Kentucky District Council
Assemblies of God

"Pastor Howard Cummings blessed my life in many ways, not only as a pastor and visionary, but in challenging me to respond to missions at an early age. Now we are challenging Argentina to do the same, with those same principles I learned years ago. The passion behind these principles is for a new generation, not just one that is in the past!"

Rev. Bradley Walz
Executive Director — Argentina
Foreign Missions Department

"Over many years, Pastor Howard Cummings was an esteemed friend of ICI University (now Global University). He shared his strong ministry with the world through our video outreach programs and supported us generously. Throughout his life, he has inspired churches to be immersed in the task of reaching the entire world for Christ.

Because of this, the words "pastor" and "missions" always will characterize his life, ministry, and vision. It is indeed fitting that he should be the one to compile the missionary messages in this excellent book."

Dr. George M. Flattery
President, Network211
President, Global University

"When I met Howard and Margie Cummings, I realized that these people don't just speak and teach about missions — they live missions! Their ministry in Moldova was not just of coming and going, but of coming and staying and bringing great fruits for His Kingdom.

CUMMINGS — it simply means be ready because they are coming with the Good News message to your place, your nation."

Bishop Victor Pavlovski
Pentecostal Union of Moldova

"The first check Howard ever wrote as a teenager was his missionary offering to send our family to Nicaragua. He has dedicated his life and ministry to the cause of reaching our generation with the Good News. His "missions credentials" are surely recorded in heaven. The churches he pastored became strong missionary churches. He and his dear wife, Margie, have traveled the world encouraging God's people everywhere toward personal and literal obedience to the Great Commission.

This compilation of messages from "missionary statesmen" is just one more way Howard Cummings is pushing to keep our generation involved in the harvest all over God's green earth. The call of his soul is this truth: If Jesus died for the whole world, then the whole world must find out what happened at Calvary. Thank you, Howard, servant of the Harvest Master."

Rev. Loren Triplett
Executive Director (Retired)
Assemblies of God Foreign Missions

"I commend you for your compilation of a great book of missions sermons entitled "THEY STILL SPEAK!" I believe this book will encourage many to respond to fulfill the Great Commission."

Dr. Peter Ong
Missions Director
Malaysia Assemblies of God

"Howard Cummings not only preaches missions but does missions. Calvary Church was greatly inspired and motivated even though it is a missions giving and sending church in Kuala Lumpur, Malaysia. One of the best Faith Promise giving Sundays was when he came and preached for us."

Rev. Dr. Prince Guneratnam
Senior Pastor, Calvary Church
Kuala Lumpur, Malaysia

"Pastor Howard and Margie Cummings have an effective, dynamic, inspirational ministry. They minister for our church on a regular basis. Experienced in missions, family life, pastoral ministry and solid in Bible teaching, they will, as with this interesting book, be a great blessing!"

Rev. Dr. David Lim
Senior Pastor
Grace Assembly of God — Singapore

"In your hands, you have the heart of nine men; my Dad and eight others just like him. These men, as General Superintendent Thomas Zimmerman used to say, were 'tall timber!' Each served, sometimes facing difficult and dangerous challenges. Each has been called home to His side. Yet, in their leaving, they still speak!"

Mr. Keith Godbey
United Airlines Pilot/Retired
Son of Missionary Ken Godbey

Philip and Virginia Hogan with James Richard and Phyllis Lynne as they left for missionary service in China, 1945.

DR. J. PHILIP HOGAN

Dr. J. Philip Hogan and his wife, Virginia, first went to China as missionaries in February of 1947, after serving churches in Springfield, Missouri; Painesville, Ohio; and River Rouge, Michigan. In Ningpo, he taught in a Bible school, supervised a church building project, and engaged in evangelistic ministry. When civil unrest, the forerunner of the communist revolution, forced the Hogans to evacuate, they moved to Taiwan (then known as Formosa). Working with another missionary couple, the Hogans founded a ministry on that island before the increasing threat of war caused him to send his wife and two children home to the U.S. Mr. Hogan remained another six months to stabilize the fledgling congregation.

Upon his return to the states, Dr. Hogan served as promotional director of the Division of Foreign Missions of the Assemblies of God, traveling the nation to encourage churches to expand their local missions ministry. In 1959, he was elected to serve his denomination as the Executive Director of the Division of Foreign Missions, a post he held for over 30 years. During that time, the number of foreign missionaries increased from 788 serving in 69 nations to over 1,500 missionaries serving in 120 countries. He served three terms as president of the Evangelical Foreign Missions Association and was recognized as one of the leading missiologists in evangelical ranks. Although serving his denomination and the entire evangelical community in executive missions leadership, Hogan's heart was still in China, and when relations with the United States eased, he and Mrs. Hogan were on the first Pan Am flight into Beijing in 1978 with a group of other dignitaries.

Philip Hogan belonged to God — he belonged to Virginia — he belonged to his denomination — and, in a very real sense he belonged to the nations of the world. But, those of us in Colorado would also establish our claim; Phil Hogan belonged to us! Born in Olathe, Colorado on a ranch, Mr. Hogan had Colorado in his blood. Until illness prevented it, he returned annually to hunt in the Black Canyon of the Gunnison.

The author was honored to serve with Dr. Hogan on the Foreign Missions Board of the denomination and enjoyed a long personal friendship. Dr. Hogan preached this message at Aurora First Assembly on November 2, 1975, during the first missions crusade we were privileged to lead at the church.

— H. C.

1

"PRIVILEGES AND RESPONSIBILITIES OF FRIENDSHIP"

Dr. J. Philip Hogan

I have chosen verses at random through the Old and New Testaments which bear on one particular privilege of those of us who are related to God through His blood and through the Cross:

Amos 3:7: "Surely the Lord God will do nothing, but He revealeth His secret unto His servants the prophets."

Deuteronomy 29:29: "The secret things belong unto the Lord our God; but those things which are revealed belong unto us and to our children forever that we may do all the words of this law."

John 15:14,15: "Ye are my friends, if ye do whatsoever I command you. Henceforth, I call you not servants, for the servant knoweth not what his lord doeth; but I have called you friends, for all things that I have heard of My Father I have made known unto you."

These verses indicate the amazing fact that the God of history, the God of the universe, the God of creation, the God of all wisdom, the God of all presence, the God of all power; this God is willing to divulge His secret unto His children. And, these verses say that to have this privilege, you have to recognize that you have a special relationship to God. This is highlighted in John's chapter 15 when He says that "I am no longer calling you servants," and there is a progression of relationship in John which I'll not have time to talk about this morning, but He said you are closer to Me than servants.

A servant may be in my house, he may come and go in the master's presence, he may hear mutterings of things going on, but he never is really taken into the inner circle of the family though he lives and serves there. Jesus said, "I have called you friends, that whatsoever I have learned of My Father, I am willing to make known to you."

Wherever the sharing of secrets in the Bible is talked about, it is always talked about on the basis of friendship. This is no better illustrated anywhere in the Bible than it is in the story of Abram, whom the Bible says was the friend of God. Whatever else he was, the great progenitor of faith, the first man in the family of the faithful, the man who went out having no continuing city, looking for one to come, the Book of Hebrews summed up this man's Divine relationship by saying he was "a friend of God."

The story is told in the Old Testament of how Abraham, who was a member of a Bedouin tribe, was in camp nearby the wicked cities of Sodom and Gomorrah, and it isn't hard for me to believe this from my traveling in the Middle East and probably some of yours. I am amazed in these days to get around the country and find people who are having the privilege of going to the Holy Land. If you've been there and you've gone from Jerusalem down to the Dead Sea or to Beersheba or to the Negev, and you've looked on either side of the road, you've seen these encampments of Bedouins that are exactly as they were in Abraham's time — no different. Living on this desert, you wonder how they eke out any existence at all. Their tents are hung low and look black because they are made out of the hair of black goats. This is the type of setting Abraham lived in. The Bible says

Mr. Hogan with an early Chinese convert and baptismal candidate.

the angels of God or whatever else they were, some kind of supernatural beings who represented God and I'm sure the language in Genesis is written to accommodate us, but it says that they came down because God sent them. Because the wickedness of these two wicked cities had arisen to God, He sent His emissaries down to see if it was exactly like the news heaven had. When they got there, they were near to the encampment of Abraham, the "friend of God," and they said, "This won't do. We're down here talking about destroying these cities and we haven't even talked it over with Abraham yet and he's the friend of God. What we are going to do here can only be judged as supernatural and what will God's friend think about God invading this territory without talking to him about it?"

The Bible says they did indeed show up at the doorway of Abram's encampment and began to disclose their plans. The friend of God began to intercede and lowered the price of destruction from 50 men to 10 because he could pray as God's friend. The Bible says Jesus said, "You are not servants, you are friends, and I'm not going to do anything in the world that I don't let you know about!" The tremendous privilege of being the friend of God.

This morning I want to talk to you briefly about three things: AWARENESS, AWAKENING, and AWAITING.

There is in America today a feeling that is sometimes difficult to interpret by educated and literate people, by the man on the street, by the college professor, by the newspaper, by the anchorman on the news program. The whole world senses in these days that there is an "ominous something" about to happen. The stock market feels it. All of society is penetrated by it. Wherever you go, from Bangladesh to Burma to South America, wherever people are literate at all about our world, there's a kind of creeping feeling underneath that it's gonna all happen one of these days and when I hear this, I say in a kind of smug way, "Oh, thank God, that's true and I know something about it!" I have an inside track that the people in the halls of Congress, if they don't know my Jesus, don't know anything about, for I'm His friend and He's not going to do anything in this world He didn't tell me about! This is my privilege — AWARENESS.

After the Biafra war and particularly after the first moon landing, one of America's great heralded liberals (if there ever was one!),

Dr. Henry Pitney Van Dusen, former president of Union Seminary in New York and a contributor to most of the liberal so-called Christian magazines said after the moon landing, "No problem need any longer be considered insolvable, no one's going to believe anymore that if we can sustain life on the moon, we cannot do it here on this earth." Somebody answered him and said, "I know no one who faces the facts and has taken accurate measure of the manifold symptoms of profound sickness in our society that still clings to this illusion. Denial or blindness to the harsh reality merely aggravates the illness!"

No longer is there any optimism. No longer does anyone expect a utopia; we have a mortal sickness, an illness that can bring culture and civilization to its close.

Would you believe that one of the world's greatest historians, a double history major from Harvard who happens to be the Secretary of State right now, Dr. Henry Kissinger, sometime ago was put this question directly: "Do you believe and can you predict the end of our civilization?" He replied, "As a historian, you would know that I have to know that you would now have to predict that our kind of society would not last much longer!" As another historian has said, "You would have to be conscious of the fact that every civilization that ever existed has ultimately collapsed!"

In the face of this, you and I have such promises as "You are not children of the darkness or of the night, but you are children of the day and of the light." God wants us to be aware, not only as His children but as His friends, of the kind of world we live in. We face this in missions all the time. Your pastor faces it with us. He joins us three times a year and faithfully serves on the Foreign Missions Board, and I want to thank you here for sparing your pastor to us for these trips. You cannot separate great world spiritual factors from great world political factors. You never have — never have been able to. The church had hardly got its footing until it was influenced by great world political factors growing out of the collapse of the Roman Empire. I have been on the phone the last three weeks it seems almost interminably. We've just had a briefing in the State Department in Washington a week ago. We've been talking about Mozambique. All of our missionaries are out of Mozambique. We've been discussing Beirut. All of our missionaries are out of Beirut. You cannot separate great world spiritual factors from great world political factors. This does not, by any stretch of the imagination, mean that the Gospel no longer operates there or that the Grace of God no longer works there, but it does mean that we need to be aware of what's in our world and understand this because God expects us to be children and friends who know what He's doing in His world!

This awareness will bring us to one tremendous conclusion and that conclusion is that there is an unprecedented AWAKENING in our world today! The irony with the great epic is that sometimes you live through it and don't know it until it's over! I'm criss-crossing the country and the world to say to people that we are living in a great spiritual epic. I wouldn't have time today or 10 days like this to document all I know about this, but I have to stand here and tell you that I'm kind of an authority. I fly 100,000 miles a year. I debrief missionaries every day. I read their correspondence. I collect their cables every morning. I move in a circle of mission executives who are as burdened as I am; and I must tell you that if I answered all the calls that come to my desk to go to conventions and seminars to tell people about the Pentecostal penetration that's in the world today, I wouldn't get anything else done! We live in a moment of tremendous spiritual awakening. I was going through a hotel in Kansas City recently and heard my name mentioned, and I looked over and there sat a friend of mine of many, many years. He said, "Come over here, Brother Hogan. I know you're in a hurry, but I want to say something to you." I went over and sat down beside him. It was Dr. George Peters, one of the leading missiologists of our time who's written the best book on the theology of missions to come out in 25 years. He's Professor of Missions at Dallas Theological Seminary and a close friend of many years. I sat down beside him and he was already crying! He said, "Phil, I only have one regret; that I'm not 37 instead of 67."

I said, "Dr. Peters, what's on your mind?" He replied, "You know, this is my sabbatical year. My university has given me money to travel the world and see what's going on so I can come back and close my career as a teacher of missions." He went on, "There's an Indian graduate student in our seminary, and I gave him money to go to India. You speak their language, you're their culture, you know these people; tell us if what we hear is going on in India really true. He came back the other day and I asked him about it. He said, 'Dr. Peters, it's not like we thought; it's ten times more than that! All over India, in villages, in rural areas, in far-off places, there are cells of believers. There are home Bible studies and prayer meetings going on in scores of places!' A sovereign move of the Spirit of God was taking place in a benighted land like India!"

Dr. Peters continued, "I went to Japan, and I went first to the Japanese Christian Council and asked how many Christians there are in Japan. They replied, 'About 900,000.'" This would coincide with my own research. He said, "I went to the Japanese Census Bureau." Japan is the most regimented society in the world. They take a census every five years. Every policeman knows every family on his block and there's one for every block. He said, "I want to know how many Christians you say there are in your country." They told him, "There are two and a half million!" He said, "Phil, I went to find them and I found them in little villages, in mountain places, in big cities, in fishing colonies, wherever they are, I found them. Sovereign cells where people have touched the Lord Jesus Christ." Most of them are not structured; most of them are not identified with any of the great names of world Christianity, but they have a simple faith and they have touched the hem of His garment!

The hallmark of the world's religious scene today, hear me people, is that there is in our world a sovereign ripening of the harvest and harvest is recognized — it's not produced, it's recognized. Jesus said, "Look on the fields that are white unto harvest." The angel of Revelation said, "The harvest of the whole world is ripe." I want to tell you this morning, members of the Body of Christ in this church, that God has brought you to the most spectacular moment to serve Him the world has ever known!

The past year and a half I've probably preached in half dozen fine churches like this which have outstanding numerical growth. Each of these pastors I've known for years. They are fine men. I've known every church they've ever pastored. They've had good ministry; never spectacular, but good ministry. Suddenly, they are pastoring churches that they can't build fast enough to contain the numbers, and I've said to these men, "What did it?" They've said, "Brother Hogan, you know as well as I do, we are sitting back and watching God do it. We're not doing much different than we've done but suddenly there's a sovereign moving of the Spirit of God."

I was in Yugoslavia recently and these poor limited people who don't hear much news from the outside, although rumors fly

The author interviews Dr. Hogan on the "Mission Possible" TV program upon his return from China in 1978.

through that Eastern Europe Russian-dominated country. You wouldn't believe it. They said, "Rev. Hogan, just tell us, just tell us please one miracle that you yourself have seen. We read and we hear all this business, and we just don't know what to think about it. Just tell us one miracle that you yourself have seen and we'll believe you." I said, "Sit down and listen to me!"

I live in a small suburban area outside the little Midwestern city of Springfield, Missouri. My neighbors aren't close. We went out to get away from neighbors, although they are getting closer to us all the time. It happens around every city. I don't know these people very well; I'm too busy and they're too busy. I know their names, I see it on their mailbox, but most of us are like most busy American communities. Down the road and around the corner from me there is a family, a couple that I know as retired people. I speak to them; they speak to me. I know that she has maintained some interest in retirement and has a little ceramic shop. I don't know anything about their religion. I don't know if they had any or a lot of it — I don't know that much about them, I'm sorry to tell you. The other day my wife went down to this little ceramic shop. She doesn't go very often; shower gift or something. She touched the door and the door fell open in front of her. The lady of the shop said to her, "Well, Sister Hogan, come in and sit down." My wife said to herself, "Well, that's strange. I've been here several times and she's never called me 'Sister' before."

The lady said, "Wait until I take care of this customer, I want to talk with you." She invited her into the back room of the shop and said, "Look at me, Mrs. Hogan." My wife looked at her and said, "I've not seen you for several weeks." She said, "Do you see anything different about me?" Mrs. Hogan said, "Yes, I believe I do. You are different. What is it?" She replied, "Don't you remember, I had one blind eye." My wife confided in me afterward, "I remember that woman. She had one eye that was drawn over in the corner and distorted; kind of an ugly feature on an otherwise very beautiful face for an older woman." She said, "I want to tell you the story. To make a long story short, my daughter introduced me to a great devotional book. She called me one night and said, 'Mother, I'm going to send you something that will help you.'"

"My daughter sent me this book. God taught me a relationship to praise I hadn't known. I began to praise God for the healing of this eye." And, she continued, "Look at it, Sister Hogan. The doctor says I have 20/20 vision!"

There's a lot to this story I haven't had time to tell you. But, I told these Yugoslavian brethren this around a table in the dining room of a little Bible school in Zagreb. They said, "Rev. Hogan, is that lady your neighbor? Did that actually happen?" I replied that I had told my wife, "Get that woman over here for coffee. I want to talk to these people myself." They came over, we had coffee, and there she sat. A Methodist for 35 years; not saved, and she said, "Brother Hogan, God healed me, saved me, and filled me. Thirty five people in my little Methodist church, including my preacher, got saved!"

Awakening! It's in our world. It's all over the world. I don't have time to tell you more. I could tell you about a simple little Catholic student who came out of Bolivia to Los Angeles to study. He went to a crusade in Springfield recently and God touched him and healed him. He went again on a recent Sunday and couldn't get in, but he was so full of what God had done for him he got a box out in the parking lot and began to preach all he knew, which wasn't much! But, it was enough. What happened inside began to happen outside and he went back to Bolivia and went from his home village until he filled the largest soccer field in that country of Bolivia! Today, a tide of revival has swept that land. It's been a tough field for us, but where we used to have four churches around the capital, we've now got 54! All because of an unbelievable, unimaginable, sovereign moving of the Holy Spirit of God!

Hear me, friends. This is the moment in history to strike for the harvest to AWAIT for His Son from heaven. God has only one thing in mind; I want to tell you this. He has only one thing in mind. Getting the world ready for His coming! The world is not going to get better politically. Get that out of your system; it's not going to be better. There is not going to be stability in the globe. If you're looking for stability in the future, you just as well forget it. It'll never be. Bad men are not going to suddenly get better. The Bible doesn't hold up this hope. The Bible says, "Wicked men will wax worse and worse, deceiving and being deceived until the end comes." The 24th chapter of Matthew is not a progression of things better, but a declination of things worse. It gets so bad He has to come back!

But, before He comes it says, "This Gospel of the Kingdom shall be preached into all the world for a witness, then shall the end come." God never sent a selfish revival to anybody. God never revives without intending that the blessing be passed on! That's the reason why you unlock the gates of God's dynamic power when you begin to do something about God's great burden in this generation; **telling the lost about Jesus!**

DR. MARK BUNTAIN

One of the best known missionaries of the 20th Century, Dr. Mark Buntain labored in Calcutta, India for over 35 years until his death in 1989. His dear wife, Huldah, personally shared with me that when they first arrived by ship, coming up the river to dock at Calcutta, her husband went to the rail and, overcome with the stench, vomited over the side. Turning to her, he declared that they would remain with their baby, Bonnie, for the brief evangelistic assignment for which they had come in 1954, a two month journey on three different ships! Then, they would leave. God, of course, had other plans and he stayed a lifetime. By the time of his death, he had founded "Mission of Mercy" hospital, a state-of-the-art medical facility in that city now serving over 100,000 patients a year, a successful day school program where literally thousands of young Indians have received their education, a trade school, numerous orphanages and children's homes, a fleet of mobile clinics in response to the overwhelming need, an intertribal church of some 3,000 souls and seven languages, and a feeding program for the poor that provides the only nutrition each day for over 25,000 street orphans and widows. His and Huldah's ministry resulted in the establishment of over 700 churches in 11 Indian states, 100 schools and Bible colleges and a global impact reaching untold numbers of people. Dr. Huldah Buntain and her daughter, Bonnie Long, continue giving leadership today to Calcutta Mercy Ministries.

Dr. Buntain delivered this moving message at Aurora on Easter Sunday, March 26, 1978.

— H. C.

Mark and Huldah Buntain with daughter, Bonnie, as they began their missionary career in Calcutta.

2

"MANY RELIGIONS — ONLY ONE JESUS!"

Rev. Mark Buntain

I'm so happy that I can tell you that Jesus is wonderful! I'm reading in the Gospel of Matthew and it is the last chapter. The wonderful scripture is what Pastor has already shared with us today — verse 6 — "He is not here for He is risen!"

About 40 miles south of the Nepal border, you will find a place called Gorakhpur and if you were to visit there, you will find that it is where Buddha is supposed to be buried. Siddhartha Gautama, who was known as the Buddha, which means the "wise one." His tomb is longer than this whole sanctuary. I don't suppose that he needed all that room, but anyway, they've got a great big grave there that's at least as long as this sanctuary. The incense is burning and the flowers are there and it's so dark. The whole scene just breaks your heart.

If you were to visit Mecca in Saudi Arabia today, they would show you the golden room where supposedly Muhammad is buried.

No one can show you where Krishna is buried because Krishna is a fake. There never was a Krishna. He's a fabled person.

But, oh people, when you look at the facts of it all; weigh it up along side story upon story and truth upon truth, you'll understand why I am so thankful for Jesus. Jesus is real. He was really crucified. He was really buried. And, as we celebrate today on this

Easter Sunday, He really rose from the dead! Jesus is alive! Amen!! This morning let's consider how wonderful Jesus is.

Jesus said in Matthew 28:19 — "Go ye therefore, and teach all nations, baptizing them in the Name of the Father, and of the Son, and of the Holy Ghost."

Do you know why Hinduism has not come to America years ago? Why it's only now that the Maharishi has brought this idea of transcendental meditation over to the United States? I'll tell you why. It is because real Brahmanism, which is the essence of Hindu teaching, says that you are not to cross the ocean to share your message or your experience with anybody else. There is no evangelism in Hinduism. There is no evangelism in pure Brahmanism. If you are a real Brahmin, you are supposed to hide it in yourself and keep everything inside. Only Christianity teaches that we are to share what we have in our Savior with others around us.

Hallelujah! Isn't that beautiful? Other religions speak of their "lords;" other religions speak of their "kings." The Bhagavad Gita is purported to be a combination of a conversation between Lord Krishna and King Arjuna, but when you read on a little bit, you discover the whole thing is a fable. Oh, but listen friends, my Bible says in Revelation 19 that "Jesus is King of Kings and Lord of Lords." Hallelujah! Only Jesus is a combination of both. He's the "Maharaja-ishwarah." He is the King of Kings and Lord of Lords. Hallelujah! I defy any Hindu; I defy any Buddhist to show me any personality in their religious thinking that is a combination of the two. Only Jesus is King of Kings and Lord of Lords.

Jesus said, "Go ye therefore, and teach all nations, baptizing them in the name of the Father, and of the Son, and of the Holy Ghost." Oh, this is beautiful!

Only Christianity has the concept of the Fatherhood of God. In Hinduism, there is no fatherhood. In Hinduism, God is a negative person, a negative idea. But, I'm thankful that Jesus said, "Lo, I have come to do the will of My Father." Hallelujah!! Only in Christianity do you have the Fatherhood of God and of the Son. Praise the Lord! Only Christianity teaches the Sonship of the believer. Only Christianity. Hinduism, at its best, will only lead you back to yourself. It teaches that you are "god" and, therefore, you begin with "god" and end with "god," and that beginning is in yourself. Therefore, you are back where you started! So, the best description of Hinduism is "zero." Believe me, it is nothing. That is the essence of it; it is nothing. Everything begins with zero and goes back to zero and so that is all you have in Hinduism. Buddhism is the very same way. I'm thankful, friend, that in the geometry of religion, when you come to Christianity you have a beautiful TRIANGLE! You have the Father, the Son, and the Holy Spirit. Amen! All worked out by Grace to satisfy my body, my soul, and my spirit.

Pastor Cummings presents a check for his mission to Dr. Buntain before his message on Easter Sunday, 1978.

Oh, this is just too big to go into this morning, but friend I'm thankful to my heavenly Father that when you come to the scientific application of this and even the mathematical conclusions of God's Book, He's not behind one bit. He will stand up in the classroom just as well as He will stand up in church! He'll stand up in the crucible of life just as much as He will stand at this holy altar this morning. He'll be just as real in your room tomorrow morning — in your office, in your factory, on the road in your car; He'll be just as real tomorrow as He is right now! Praise the Lord! Oh, I love Him for this and friend, I'm so glad that this beautiful Christ is filled with compassion.

This is a beautiful Bible word. You will not find compassion in the other religions. There are two words that you will not find in the essence of Hinduism or Buddhism. One is forgiveness and the other is compassion. They are not there. You'll discover that in modern Hinduism they have picked up the word forgiveness, but they borrowed it from the Christians! In essence, it is not there. Forgiveness is a Bible word, and so is compassion.

When I arrived in Calcutta nearly 25 years ago, I looked upon that mass of humanity and it was the precious children that broke my heart. I started, by God's Grace, to take care of many thousands of these precious youngsters. We started a feeding program to many of these precious boys and girls. In the middle of this past year, the order was passed that these vagrant children were supposed to be cleaned off the streets of our city and during the night, the big trucks would go by and gather up the garbage that is simply thrown out into the road. The big lorrys went by and gathered up the garbage and the policemen followed behind and picked up the children! They took them outside the city to a place called "Bantola." While they shoved the garbage into one pile, the children were pushed up behind.

The Police Commissioner came to me and said, "Would you go out and try to help; would you try to do something for these boys and girls?" It has been a joy to work with these precious youngsters.

We have a program to give them one nutritious meal of bread and milk each day. The fact is, they are not allowed to take food home or take it into the street. They have to eat it where they are because someone would take it from them. So, they eat the food there at the city dump!

One morning, I saw this little boy. He had a plate of vegetable curry and rice beside him. His arm was up on the table; they eat with their hands. He was pushing the food silently under his arm. Then, I noticed that he would take it and stuff it into the little pocket in his shirt. I came around behind him and laid my hand on his shoulder. When he looked up with his big eyes, he thought I was going to scold him. I said, "Sonny, why are you putting food in your pocket?" "Sir," he said, "I'm taking it home to my father. He's hungry."

Dear friend, I can talk to you this morning about many heartaches. I can share with you the realities of what God sees on the other side of the world. One-fourth of my country goes to bed hungry every night. I am thankful that there are many ways in which great progress has been made, but still, in a country where 21 million babies will be born this year and one million will not reach their fifth birthday; where two-thirds of them will never see their eighteenth birthday. Dear friends, there is another world out there that God sees! There is another world out there that He loves, and I'm so thankful for the privilege of being able to serve Him. He is a wonderful Christ of compassion.

Mark and Huldah Buntain established Mission of Mercy, a global ministry of church planting, Christian education, and humanitarian work.

God spoke to my heart in 1968. I was moving amongst this hospital and I saw its heartaches. We were able to open our own hospital program, step-by-step, and we are very, very thankful. I'm just coming back from Calcutta. I've been back now about six weeks, and on a Monday morning before I came to America a gentleman came to see me. As he sat at our breakfast table, he said, "There is one thing I want you to do for me. I would be grateful if you will do this."

I said, "What's wrong?"

He said, "In Madras, there is a very lovely Christian family. They are very poor people. They have a little girl three years of age who is badly crippled. She cannot walk. Can you help her?" I said, "I'm sure we can. They'll have to hurry though because I have to leave."

I went to the phone and called one of the relatives and said, "Bring the little girl. Get her up here as quickly as you can."

They came to the city and they stayed in our own apartment. She is a darling little girl. Three years of age — an obvious polio case — we took her over to our hospital. I have some splendid orthopedic physicians working with me and after the examination, it was obvious that we could make this little girl walk. I went out into the hallway where the family was waiting for me and I said to them, "Don't worry. God is going to help us. We can make your little girl walk. She is going to walk!"

I talked to them a little bit, but I could see that on their faces was a big question mark. How much is this going to cost us? I said, "You don't need to worry now. This is not going to cost you anything. This is the Lord's work. You leave the baby here. We are going to take good care of your child. This won't cost you a thing. Her mother can stay here. The baby will be about four months with us and she can stay right here. We'll help you."

I was able to send that precious Christian family back to Madras. We have the little girl and by God's Grace, we'll put her on her feet. She is going to walk. Hallelujah!

Dear ones, this makes Easter real. The symbols are all glorious and beautiful and I thank God for them, but this is the real Easter! Jesus is alive and He works in our hearts so that we share His love and compassion. We share in His ministry.

The story I'm about to share is unbelievable; the true account of a priest of Nepal out of the Royal Family who took a child bride. Oh, I wish I could take this little girl's life and put it deep into your heart. India has arranged marriages and these little girls are set up to be married before they even reach the age of fourteen. For this child bride, her case is even more tragic. Her husband died. It used to be that a young widow was burned alive on the same pile of wood as that which cremated her husband's body, but by law that practice is now prohibited. However, the stigma remains.

This young girl was under the curse of the belief that some sin in her life had caused her husband's death. Therefore, she began to search through her books trying to find a way for her salvation. She was informed by her Hindu studies that if she would make a journey to the five principal shrines of India she could find salvation. She came to our city of Calcutta. She stayed in the Hindu Temple to Kali, the goddess of death and destruction after whom the city of Calcutta is named. She wept and she prayed asking Kali to do something to relieve her guilt. She then went to the Temple of Jagannath in the city of Puri; from there to Madurai and there in front of the big stone Goddess of Meenakshi she pled and pled, but nothing happened. She finally went to Banaras, the capital city of the Hindu people on the banks of the Ganges and she wept and prayed. To add to her penance and her torment, she built five fires and sat in the middle of the intense heat of that flame under the sun out in the middle of the courtyard. When winter time came, she sat in a pool of icy water up to her chin trying her best to atone and pay for the sin of being guilty of her husband's death.

That dear girl found no peace in the heat of the summer or in the cold of the winter until one afternoon she went into the bazaar and someone handed her the Gospel of John. She took it home and began to read it and for the first time in her life, Chandalina discovered there is a God Who really loves her. She gave her life to Jesus Christ. Her life was completely changed! She gathered up her false gods and went to her priest. She said, "Here, take these things. I've served them all my life and they have done me no good." Chandalina became one of the finest lady evangelists in India!

Friend, this morning I'm glad that my Jesus is alive. His is the love that He gave to me. His is the power that set me free and I'm thankful today my Savior is alive. Amen! Oh, beloved, let the Spirit of God in Christ Jesus captivate your soul today and know that regardless of what the situation is, regardless of where you are, I can assure you that Jesus Christ is a friend that sticks closer than a brother. He said, "I will never leave you nor forsake you. Call upon Me in the day of trouble and I will deliver thee and thou shalt glorify Me."

He is simply wonderful. I have proved it time and again, there are many religions but there is **ONLY ONE JESUS**!

The Africans named Mr. Plotts "Bwana Tembo," which means "Lord or Mister Elephant."

REV. MORRIS PLOTTS

"Bwana Tembo"

Morris Plotts went into foreign missionary service at a point in life when most men are entering retirement. Told initially by the leadership of his denomination that he was too old for appointment, he first went at his own expense. Later, the missions department acquiesced and gave him official endorsement; he would continue missionary service until well into his eighties.

Perhaps no individual missionary impacted my life more than Brother Plotts. As a boy, I would go with the church group in an old rickety former Council Bluffs, Iowa city bus my father had purchased, to Griswold, Iowa to assist Evangelist Plotts in founding a new congregation, using a rented old theater building for services. I would sit on the front row totally mesmerized, watching the man's size 16D shoes, as he paced back and forth on the stage, preaching. It was later my honor to host Missionary Plotts several times in our pulpit in Colorado.

Known affectionately as "Bwana Tembo" (Lord Elephant) by the East Africans because of his large stature, Morris Plotts was an exceptionally brilliant preacher. The classic sermon, "Twenty-Sixth Row," is a message where he depicts graphically what Charles Swindoll described in one of his books: "How easy to be spoiled… presumptuous… sassy… ungrateful…when our spiritual stomachs are full! Funny thing — those who are full usually want more. We belch out increased demands rather than humble gratitude to God for our horn o' plenty." (1)*

---

*(1) — Taken from *Growing Strong in the Seasons of Life* by Charles R. Swindoll. Copyright © 1983 by Charles R. Swindoll, Inc. Used by permission of Zondervan, pg. 195.

We include two messages by Morris Plotts. He preached "The Twenty-Sixth Row" in Aurora on April 24, 1983. "Sharing the Warranty," (or "What Is A Missionary?") was delivered on November 4, 1979.

— H. C.

3

"THE TWENTY-SIXTH ROW"

Rev. Morris Plotts

This morning I want to talk to you from what I think is one of the most beautiful scenes portrayed in all the Bible. It's so full of human need with which we are very familiar, but the beautiful part about it is the compassion of our God and the magnificence of our Christ in reaching men and meeting the needs of human beings. The story is recorded in four places in the New Testament: Matthew, Mark, Luke, and John. We'll mainly consider what we find in the Book of Mark, chapter 6. What has happened here is that the Disciples have just returned from their evangelistic tour. They had been sent forth by the Lord two by two and had completed their task. Now, they have returned to the Lord in a place called Capernaum, told Him all that they have done and how God had worked with them. The Lord, our Savior, noticing their weariness said with compassion, "Let's come apart and rest awhile."

So, at His instruction, they clamored aboard a little ship and Jesus climbed aboard with them. Then, Jesus with the Twelve, started to make their way across the northern reaches of the Sea of Galilee to a wilderness place called desert most of the year because of the dry time, but in the spring of the year, which it was at this time, it was lush with green grass. They proceeded to this wilderness place where there were no cities, no milling crowds, to get away for a little time of rest. But, the crowds in the northwestern shores of the Galilee region saw our Savior and His Disciples departing and they immediately struck out by land across the northern reach of the Sea of Galilee and the result was that when they came ashore near Bethsaida, several thousands of people were there waiting for them. The Sea of Galilee, as you know, is really only a small lake, not more than eight miles at the widest. So, here were these throngs of people waiting for Jesus when He stepped ashore. I love these words written about Him: "He was moved with compassion because He saw them as sheep not having a shepherd."

The next thing that we read is that He began to minister to the people and God alone knows the wonderful things that happened that day when, from the lips of the God-man, fell these wonderful words of truth. Sick were healed, devils were cast out, men were delivered from their distresses and troubles. It was a beautiful, beautiful day and a day of victory for the Kingdom of God. But now the day is far spent and the weary sun begins to hang low over the hills of Naphtali westward and the Twelve Disciples, like a good board of concerned deacons, because that's really the way they acted in their ministry with the Lord; always serving the Lord and helping Him, going here and there arranging things, were concerned about the people. I appreciate this about them; they were very concerned, as the day was far spent and here were thousands of people there on that hillside where Jesus had ministered to them. Remember, it was a wilderness place and there was no place to buy food, and in their haste to get to the meeting, they had not brought food with them and I appreciate their concern.

I can overhear the Disciples talking: "There's got to be something done about this crowd of people. They've brought nothing to eat and they are hungry. The children will be crying and screaming for bread; the old will be faint and famished and perhaps faint by the wayside. We'd better get this crowd off our hands; we'd better get rid of them."

This is pretty much a disciple's way of solving a problem. At least I've found it so often in my own life. My attempts sometimes to solve a problem have been to get the problem out of sight and out of mind! That doesn't solve the problem. Sweeping it under the carpet isn't exactly the way to get the right answer.

So, the Disciples, in their concern, wanted to get the crowd off their hands; out of sight and out of mind. Finally, they came to the Savior and said, "Lord, these people don't have anything to eat. There are thousands of people here and no where to procure bread. Please send them away."

I'm amazed at what Jesus said; not as amazed as they were, of course, but Jesus said to them: "You feed them!"

"What? We are to feed them? Lord, talk sense." They are so much as saying, "Talk sense. How will we feed them? What little lunch we brought along for our day off wouldn't go anywhere with this crowd of thousands of people. How can we feed them?"

And Jesus said, "How many loaves do you have?" I'm sure they protested that they only had their own tiny lunch. "We don't have any. How can we feed them, Lord? How can we feed them?"

Jesus said, "You go and see!"

The Disciples immediately made their way into the surging, milling crowd of now hungry people, late in the afternoon on that wonderful day out on the hillside and they found, glory be!, a little boy, praise God, who had his lunch!

Now, that puts a strain on my faith, ladies and gentlemen. I believe everything in this Book from Genesis to Revelation, but it does strain my faith nevertheless to think that this lad would have his lunch at five o'clock in the afternoon! I know young folks, we raised six healthy, strong children in our family, and I can tell you the truth that mashed potatoes, mounds of mashed potatoes, can disappear like snowballs in a furnace with hungry kids around. You know, that kindly mama or auntie or grandma had said, "Our little laddie's going running off to that revival today. He'll be hungry before he gets back."

So, they put him up a lunch of five pancake shaped barley loaves, two small dried fish, and probably wrapped, as is the custom in that part of the world, in a banana leaf. And, the little fellow still had his lunch at five in the afternoon! It strains my faith, but then, I think it perhaps was this way. Such wonderful things happened that day. Such wonderful things! And, when the Spirit of the Lord is moving, we do find ourselves caught up in a way out of temporalities into the things of the Divine and spiritual world and that's a wonderful time, isn't it? Doubtless that is what happened that day, so that the little fellow forgot all about his lunch.

There it was, late in the afternoon and Andrew found him. I want to pay tribute to that little fellow. He surrendered his lunch to the Apostles. What about that? That is point number two that I think is remarkable, and they brought it to Jesus.

The Lord Jesus now told the Disciples, "Make these people sit down in the grass."

You know, it is important that in everything there should be order because one of heaven's first laws is order. This is a universe of order and the Lord Jesus was not about to have those disciples milling around like so many hogs at a trough! Thousands of them. So, He said, "Have them sit down by companies on the grass."

The women and children would have been on one side in Oriental fashion; the men on the other. I like the way that it's described with such care by Mark who describes the incident this way: "They were made to sit down in the grass by companies, by hundreds and fifties."

For a long time I pondered over the meaning of those words and then I came to the conclusion that it must be that they were seated in rows, by companies of 100 and 50. A 100 in a row and 50 rows would make 5,000. That is the number of the men that was given as the number seated on the hillside in the grass by rows and by companies. But when I discovered in the Greek text of the New Testament and Mark's Gospel, when I discovered that the very Greek word used to describe how they were seated in the grass is the word "Prasia," which is the word for a row in a vegetable garden, I said, "Praise God! That hunch wasn't wrong after all; it was the truth!" Mark puts it this way: "They were seated "prasia." Mark 6:40 — "ranks." Rows-rows-rows — they were seated prasia! There they are, seated upon the hillside in rows by companies; 100 in a row and 50 rows or, if you will have it the other way, 50 in a row and 100 rows, but I believe that it probably was 100 in a row and 50 rows.

And now, the Lord Jesus commands His Disciples to procure baskets. No problem! Baskets were as common there as billfolds and shopping bags are to us here and they bring some baskets to the Lord. Now, the Disciples stand before Him. What is next? Jesus takes the little boy's lunch of five barley loaves and two fish, looks up to heaven and gives God thanks. He who bringeth forth bread from the earth and, after His prayer of thanksgiving, our Savior takes those barley loaves and begins to crumble them into fragments, dropping them into the empty baskets. He takes the fish, breaks the pieces of dried fish and crumbles them. The crumbling pieces of fish and loaves tumble into the baskets. But, there is something happening! Please don't ask me to explain. All I know is that something unusual happened. That's all I can tell you for sure. I can't tell exactly how it happened, but I can tell you it did happen. For all of a sudden, something's happening to those crumbs and those broken fish and those broken loaves of bread. Molecules are multiplying and there is bread and fish coming into those baskets until they stand now with their baskets full of bread and fish! Please, if I may, MIRACLE bread and fish! Don't be surprised because the fingers that broke bread that day are the same fingers that tossed this world out into space in ages past and that isn't all. Don't forget it, He streaked the sable heavens with the Milky Way and spangled those skies with blazing lights. For the Bible declares that all things were made by Him and one of the most careful and implicit and consistent teachings in the whole New Testament is that God, through Christ, created all things. All things were made by Him and the Maker of worlds broke bread that day and multiplied that bread and fish.

Now the time comes for the Disciples to begin their ministry. And, by the way, here is a beautiful lesson. God is the supplier of all our needs, but always, there are the intermediaries. God could do it directly by Himself; He doesn't have to lean upon angels as crutches. He doesn't have to depend upon men. But God could, if He pleased, do what He wills to do. He could speak the word and it's done. He could speak a word and fill every stomach in this world in one instant of time. That isn't God's way. Always, God's way is the need; He is the supplier of the need, He is pleased to take into His fellowship and into His service men that will do His will and obey His call and His bidding. There is that intermediary. There is the ministry He has been pleased to share with us. It is a privilege and it is an honor. Blessed be God!

So, the Disciples now begin their ministry of miracle bread and fish to those hungry multitudes. Oriental fashion, it's of course the men first. I don't agree with it, I don't vote that way at all, but that's the way it is over there; still is — men first. So, I see the Apostles now start down the long front row. There are 100 in that row. Fifty rows of hungry men seated in the grass. Peter, James, John, Matthew, Andrew, Thomas, and, yes, Judas is there — all of them. Baskets full of miracle bread and fish. I can see Peter saying to that hungry Hebrew, "Would you like some bread?" And John saying, "Would you like some fish?"

And, the people don't have any manners! They are grabbing; they've never read anything by Emily Post. Hungry they are; ill-mannered they are; uncouth they are, and I see them, as the Apostles go down that front row, ministering bread and fish to those hungry men. It isn't long until they have fish grease all over their faces, crumbs upon their lips. Now, to row two, and row three, row four, row five. I see them back at row 10, now they are back at row 12; they've arrived at row 22, 50 rows of 100 in a row. Now, they are at row 24 and I find them at row 25. Bread and fish served and those hungry Hebrews are reaching out and grabbing.

Morris and Neva Plotts as they appeared near the conclusion of their illustrious missionary career.

And, now I'm going to ask permission as I reach row 25 in our story. Up to now, we've been accurate, we've been careful, we've brought you the scene as it was upon the hill-side that day. But, you know, I'm a guest in this church this morning and I'm delighted to be the guest of your lovely pastor, my dear friend, Brother Cummings, and never would I have anything to say in any church anywhere without the full permission of the pastor, the official board, the trustees, the officials of every kind in the church and the people of this communion! First of all, I would ask my pastor for permission to do something in this pulpit this morning. I've told you the absolute truth thus far, but at this juncture, I ask my pastor for permission to tell a lie in this pulpit!!

(In the background, Pastor Cummings is heard saying, "Go ahead!" Laughter follows.)

Well, thank you. Thank you. I should appeal to the official board next, but I think your pastor probably speaks the sentiments of the board. I remember recently in Visalia, California, my friend Ernest Kumpe was on the platform and with about 1,000 people out there, and I spoke along this line, stopped and asked him for permission to tell a lie in his pulpit and he look startled. The people began to laugh and he said, "Proceed with caution!"

And, thus it shall be. The reason I want to tell a lie in this pulpit this morning will be very evident in just a little bit, and please don't say that this funny guy from Louisiana tried to deceive us, because I'm not deceiving you. I warned you it isn't true. I've given you every warning possible that this is not true, but I'm telling it for a reason. Because the lie that I want to tell is true! Now, how do you like that?

We've arrived at row 25 in the ministry of the bread and fish to those hungry men on the hillside. I promise you now that I am telling a lie. They wind their way back from row 25 to row one and those Apostles are handing now the bread and fish the second time to the hungry, greasy-faced, becrumb-lipped Hebrews! Bread and fish. More bread and fish and they are grabbing again. **Row 26 has not been served!** Row 29 has been forgotten. Row 49 has been forgotten.

They are as hungry in row 50 as they were in row one, but they are overlooked! They are forgotten. They are omitted, while the Disciples are giving the second helping to the front row, the front two rows, the front four rows. They have arrived at row 25 the second time and, now I see them. (It didn't happen. It's a lie.)

Now I see them coming back again to row one the third time. More bread; more fish. Row 26 through row 50 has not been touched! They've not been allowed to smell the miracle fish. They've not seen a crumb of that miracle bread. They're hungry. They are as faint as those on the front rows and now for the tenth time, the twentieth time, the front rows are being fed again and again and again and the back rows are being forgotten and overlooked and left alone!

Now, those on the first 25 rows are complaining! One old fellow is saying, "Did you see that rig that Peter's wearing? What a garb!" Another says, "Did you hear John's speech? He dangles his participles and splits his infinitives." Another group over here is fussing about this and that and one says, "There should be a certain color of carpet to serve bread and fish like this." Yet another remarks, "I've tasted better bread than this. I've had better fish than this!" A voice from row 24 cries out, "Hey, do you have any tartar sauce? I could use some ketchup! This stuff is bland!"

Now, these once hungry people be-served, if you please, are beginning to find fault with the servitors of the blessing, while the back rows go famished.

Ladies and gentlemen, that didn't happen. Had it happened, the Lord Jesus would have called His Apostles to Himself and said, "Brethren, you are not doing well. I made this bread. I created this fish. I did this for all these people, and you are not doing well to feed them again and again and again and leave those back rows to famish."

You know what did happen? The Bible is plain. They did ALL eat and were filled, so saith the Word of God, until the last man, woman, and child, hungry they were, but, on that hillside, they were filled by the miracle of God's Grace through the Lord Jesus. Every man, woman, and child and, so wonderful was the provision that when it was all over, the disciples were sent forth by the Master to pick up the scraps and there were 12 baskets full — leftovers after everybody had been filled. And, I don't know what you're thinking, but knowing the Lord as I've learned to know Him, I wouldn't be a bit surprised if He called His Apostles to Himself and said, "Look, take these 12 baskets of food and give them to that little boy who surrendered his lunch!"

That's the way God deals with us in His graciousness; the way He gives us, "pressed down, shaken together, and running over," when we've served Him and done His will.

But, you said, "I'm perplexed at why you told such a monstrosity! Such a completely impossible thing. Why did you tell this preposterous thing? Because that is exactly what my generation of Christians has done with the Gospel! And, I stand today with my head bowed to ask God to forgive me for my share of the corporate blame of us living in this present time and belonging to the Church worldwide. Why haven't we done what He told us to do? We could if we would.

Because I declare unto you a parable, following the lead of our blessed Savior, who taught heavenly things from the things of earth, and on that hillside that day, I want you to see the picture of thousands on the hillside seated there on the grass and a provision made for them. It's the beautiful picture we have in the Word of God where the Lord tells us in His Word that "God so loved the world, that He gave His only begotten Son," and that the plan He had was not only for just a few but for everybody! He, Who is not willing that any should perish, but that all should come to repentance!

Ladies and Gentlemen, the plan of salvation revealed in the Bible is a plan of salvation for the entire world. Not for just a particular group. Not for any select company, but for every man, woman, and child on this great planet earth.

And, you know what we've done? I declare unto you a parable. Do you know what we've done? We've done exactly like that impossible scene that I portrayed on the hillside that day, which didn't happen. But now the analogy does happen when it comes to this dispensation and the distribution of bread. It didn't happen, **but it does happen!** And I'm not far off when I say that, because Jesus at Capernaum a couple of days later explained to the people what happened out in the wilderness when He said, "Your fathers ate the bread that God sent out in the wilderness and you didn't follow Me because of the things you saw or heard because you were fed in the wilderness. But I am the true Bread that the Father has sent down from heaven, and if any man eats this Bread, he will live forever!"

Jesus Christ proclaimed Himself as the Bread of Life and we, in our generation of Christians, have done just like that impossible scene that I portrayed on the hillside at Bethsaida. We have done just that — the awful, crushing, staggering fact that I can scarcely live with!

It breaks my heart. It burdens my soul and troubles me day and night; the fact that in this world of four billion, four hundred million people, half of that number — two billion, two hundred million have never had one adequate presentation of the Gospel. That is not a figure just tossed casually and carelessly off the cuff. That is research material, a consistent discovery of students of missiology, with the signature of our own J. Phillip Hogan, Foreign Missions Director. Two billion, two hundred million. That's why, on the hillside, I put it that way! The last 25 rows forgotten, while we give bread and bread and bread and bread to those who have already received it. Why haven't we done what He told us to do?

Is it fair for me to hear the Gospel twice when there are those who have never heard it once? Is it fair for me to hear the Gospel a thousand times when millions have never heard it once? That's the thing that tore me from my pastorate. Not for one moment that we don't need pastors here, of course we do! They are God's gift, as we just heard in that beautiful Bible lesson today. God's gift to the church. We need churches like this. I honor and respect you. God gives pastors like your pastor to you and I love and honor and respect him. The fact remains that we should feed those on the front rows and feed them well. Your pastor does. But, those back rows that have never been reached with men and women going to a lost world, need to be reached too. For there is no other Name under heaven given among men whereby we must be saved.

I propose that in this day in which we live, a day of opportunities unparalleled with technology that the world has never seen, I propose that we gird up the loins of our minds. **That we set our faces to the task and take this Gospel to every man, woman, and child and do what our Savior told us to do**. He's Bread for all and we must take it to all of them or answer to Christ for having not done so. Bless you!!

Morris Plotts preached the following message in Aurora on November 4, 1979:

"WHAT IS A MISSIONARY?"
("Sharing The Warranty")

Rev. Morris Plotts

We missionaries know, and know it full well, that we would not stand a foot high if it were not for pastors like yours and people like you. The missionary can have in his heart great things that God talks about and it's true that "In the last days, saith God, I will pour out my Spirit upon all flesh. Your sons and your daughters shall prophesy. Your young men shall see visions," (I pause to give you my franchise), "your old men shall dream dreams!" (Joel 2:28) I want to assure you that God can put the vision of a young man into steel, stone, flesh and blood. He can take the dream of an old man and make it live! You know how He does it? Through wonderful people like you who become part of what God is doing in this great hour just before our Savior returns.

There's a beautiful principle found in the Bible. David was a man after God's own heart. He thought many beautiful, wonderful thoughts, just like God would think them, and there was a time when the Philistines raided their camp. David and his warriors were gone and upon their return, they found their camp in ruins. Wives and children had been abducted, their property stolen. Great was the discomfiture of David and his men. Immediately, they said, "We must go forth. We must fight with these Philistines and retrieve our possessions and get back our wives and children."

But then, there was a division made of the forces, for David said, "Some will have to stay here at the camp and some will go out to do battle." Thus they did. The battle was won; God gave the victory. The warriors with David came back flushed with victory. They had retrieved their possessions, wives, and children — brought them back home safe — and they "spoiled" the Philistines. Then, everyone began to talk about the spoils of the battle. Oh how they had that day enriched themselves, and the warriors were ready to divide it among themselves! Said they, "We went out to battle. We'll have it. It'll be ours. These that stayed home — no, no, they won't have any."

David, whose heart so many times thought the same kind of thoughts that God thought, said, "No, no. They that stayed with the stuff shall share and share alike with those who went to do battle."

Do you like that? I think it's beautiful, just like everything that God thinks. There are those of us who go to the mission field. Those many of whom you support and stand by in your great

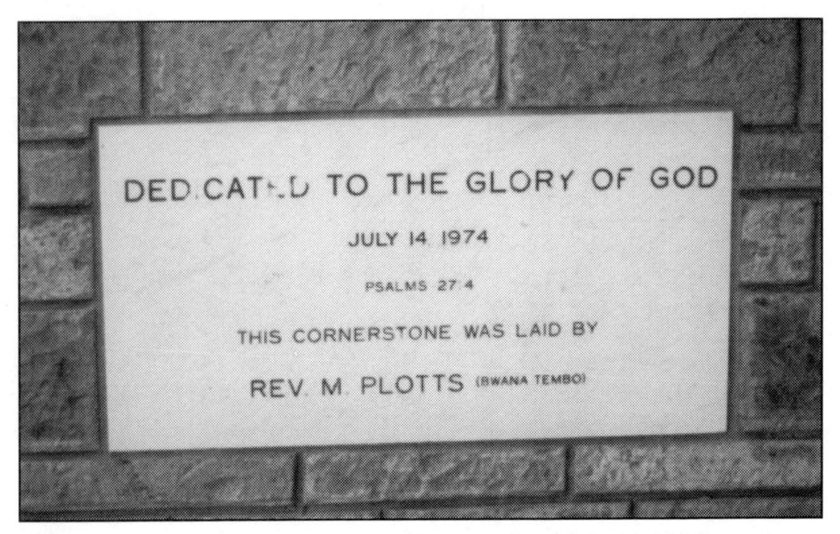

Mr. Plotts raised funds and supervised construction of church buildings on every Continent. This photo was taken by the author at Nairobi Evangelistic Center.

church here — missionaries on the far-flung fields, on the very frontiers of the Kingdom of God, if you please. There is a battle. It isn't easy, and if you think for one single minute that being a missionary is just a grand party all the time, please think differently. There are a lot of things that we can't tell you about — wouldn't tell about — but it takes everything there is in a man to be what God wants him to be, and I must tell you that many times the battle is overwhelming. To be sure, God is going to reward the missionary for leaving home, loved ones, safety of our country, the conveniences. I often times say it with a laugh just for a joke: "The one thing wrong with the place I'm building my next church in the jungle is that it is 9,000 miles from K-Mart!" I say it just for fun, but nevertheless it's true.

There are sacrifices, and compassion has its cost. Real, true compassion. The man that wrote that lovey-dovey, sweetie pie letter to his girlfriend you've probably heard about. It was filled with every kind of sweet thing that could ever be put into words. How adorable she was. How beautiful she was. How he couldn't live without her; would climb the highest mountain just to be with her; swim the widest river just to be with her. On and on and on. Signed it loves, kisses, hugs and then, "P.S., see you on Saturday night if it doesn't rain!" A lot of consecration I know has that "P.S." We'll go to the mission field if it isn't too far from K-Mart!

There will be a reward to those who have made the sacrifice, but they will not receive and enjoy that reward alone. They that have sent and stood by the stuff; they that have made it possible for the missionary's dream to come to pass and his vision to be accomplished, they will share and share alike at the great Judgment Seat of Christ — the "Bema Judgment." I read in I Corinthians 4 and 5 these illuminating words: "On that day shall every man have praise of God."

It is God saying "thanks" to His saints for doing His will, for obeying His voice and working that which was pleasing in His sight. And, you are going to share it church! Your pastor is going to share. We missionaries will not stand alone, but together we will receive a reward for having brought the Good News to men who have never heard it. Planting churches where a church was never known; taking Bibles into places where a Bible was never dreamed of, never conceived of such a book as being a Book from God. We'll be rewarded; you'll be rewarded; we'll be rewarded together! Even a cup of cold water given in the name of a disciple, Jesus said, shall not lose his reward. (Matt. 10:42)

Would you tell me what it is going to mean on that day of awards when the noble deeds done in Jesus' Name, the Name above every name, are rewarded? The Name that causes angels to hush their singing and stand in adoration; deeds done in His Name and for His sake, with motives clean and pure, that He might be pleased, shall be amply rewarded!

Well bless your darling hearts! We'll be in it together; missionaries who went and churches who sent. So, I want to thank you and commend you and congratulate you for the vision God has given your pastor and the board, those who are in control of the affairs of this great church. It is not an empty thing. It is not some wild imagination, but I'm satisfied in my heart, as I listen to the story, that it came from God. Born of God — dropped from heaven into the heart of your pastor and there isn't one smidgeon of selfishness about it, because it is beyond the four walls of this church — beyond the 12 acres of your lovely piece of land here. Beyond the city of Denver and its environs and lovely Colorado, it is to the uttermost parts of the earth. To do for them, to spend for them, to share with them, it's beautiful and God is going to reward it. Praise the Name of the Lord!

You know, the trouble with this business of ministering — can I tell you? — is that you never get through. There are a million things I want to say and can't say, but I did get started and, don't anybody be alarmed, I'm not like the fellow that the little boy described as an "escaped missionary" because he talked for hours. I'll just speak for a few minutes and tell you that missionaries are really different than many people think. So little are they understood. So few are the people that really do understand missions, but you are different. Your pastor is different. And, I know what I'm talking about when I say that in so many places, I walk among good Godly people whose hearts love Jesus and they are going to heaven. God has been so good to them and they are Christians, but they just don't understand missions. As I go among them, I'm something of a freak! They look upon me as something of an oddity. It is not just my big feet alone. It is not just the fact that I was born ugly and never got over it, but the fact that I'm a missionary. "Missionary?" They can hardly say it without a crinkle in their nose — "Missionary? What's a missionary?"

If I had the time, I would tell you some of the great errors; great flagrant errors that are cherished in the hearts of good people. These are people who are going to heaven to spend eternity with Jesus. And, they are going to live with missionaries forever in heaven, but don't understand it now but will understand it better by and by! Oh, that they could understand it now so they could be a part of all of this!

I'll just tell you that if you'll spell missionary right, it will help you to understand. I have some scholars in the audience today so I appeal to them for their assent if I'm right. Webster has it M-I-S-S-I-O-N-A-R-Y! I ask the combined, aggregate scholarship on this platform, am I right? Missionary. Well, you say, how else would you spell it? If I would spell it like most people believe, then it must be spelled M-O-O-C-H-I-N-A-R-Y. Give me, give me, give me. Bloodsucking leech! Give me, give me, give me. Why doesn't he get a job like anybody else? Why doesn't he pastor a church like our pastor? Why isn't he an evangelist? Why is he a missionary, moochinary?

I've got some news for you, friend. The missionaries I have known down through the years, I've felt that I have associated myself with royalty when I'm with them. And, we have a missionary on the platform this morning who is an official with our denomination in the Far East; the Northern Far East. Am I not right in our system of auditing? We have scrutiny from upstairs to downstairs, and I'm thankful for that! You can trust the program in our fellowship. It's clean, it is forthright, it is done properly. And, we are not, I say, we are not in the presence of God and His holy angels and the saints of God; we are not moochinaries! The missionaries who can make it to the field accomplish things for God. They make their way through those devious and difficult paths of interaction and fundraising and budgets. Put it down in your little book, like a pastor who can stay in a church, pastor that church, and feed the congregation and build the work of God; put it down in your little book, that missionary who can make it to the field and succeed has got qualities that would make him an outstanding success in many lines. If you can raise a budget, get to a foreign country, and do the job, I assure you that you could sell Chevrolets, real estate, insurance and on and on and on. If you have qualifications that will enable you to do those things by God's grace, you wouldn't have to sit around waiting for someone to give you some little odd job to do. This ministry is not made up of misfits that have nothing else they can do. But, God has laid His hand upon them; put it down in your little book! Missionaries are missionaries for reasons beyond any such carnal suggestions that they are in it for money.

Money? You say, "Well, you're always talking about thousands of dollars."

It comes in this hand and goes out this hand! Do I look like I'm fussing? Do I look like I'm growling? Do I look like a sourpuss? Do I sound to you like I'm complaining? I'm not. But missionaries, as far as we're concerned, our allowances are really on the lower end of the spectrum compared to the wages of today. Complain? If I had to sleep on a clothesline and have "wind pudding" for breakfast, I'd rather serve God as a missionary than anything I know! The satisfaction of taking the Good News to people who have never heard it. The joy of seeing faces light up when you tell them about a Savior. The joy that these people have who have lived in such hopelessness for so many years. You talk about satisfaction in life; you talk about fulfillment! I say to you in the fear of God, "Give me a chance, Lord. Lord, give me a chance. Let me go back. Keep me strong. Keep me well. I want to go back to the jungle. I want to go back to the people that I love!"

I'm not saying this for anybody to give me any credit. It's no more than I ought to do. Jesus told us when we've done what He told us to do, we've only done what we should have done and I thank Him for enabling us to do it. I'm thrilled with my life in missions.

I want you to know that we missionaries, believe it or not, are just as human as you. Not almost, but just as much. Somebody says, "Well, I don't know about that! These missionaries — one's got a halo around his head and this one over here is a freak!"

Okay, we are peculiar in our ways. Please overlook our oddities as we overlook yours. But, what I'm saying is that we are just exactly like you. Crossing, as it were, going on the other side of the counter, there is no difference between this man and you. No difference between me and these fine men sitting on the front row; no difference. Absolutely no difference. Same kind of nervous systems, bone structures; same problems and frustrations. We know what it is to be happy. We know what it is to be sad. We know what it is to be mad. "What?" you say. A missionary ever get mad? Yes. God forgives us like He does you. Same way. We're just the same. Not a speck of difference, and I've got news for you: God just takes ordinary folks and He speaks to them what He wants them to do.

There's that beautiful Scripture in Mark 13 which tells us that Jesus is like the husbandman who went off into a far country and left his goods with his servants. Then came these words: "And he gave authority to his servants and to every man his work."

Did you hear me? Every man. Every woman. It's a generic term. It stands for all humanity. Everyone of us in our work. We've got a job to do. We're not just any old Joe, Mary, Bill, or Sally. (Excuse me if I used your name!) Or, any old Morris. But, we are SOMEBODY! God called each of us to do something in His Kingdom. It may not be something that will put your name in lights on a marquee. It may not be something that will make people praise you. They may not understand you. They may know nothing about you, but to every man his work. There is a job for you to do, and when you came into the Kingdom of God at that altar, weeping your way to Christ, finding salvation on that wonderful occasion, God didn't turn around and say, "Who's that? Where did he come from?" He knew all about you and you were born into the Kingdom with a plan, bless God, and that plan is that every man has his work to do!

You know why the church has suffered? Why the cause of Christ has been hindered? Why the Kingdom of God has been slowed

Morris and Neva Plotts pause to survey the land and the people they loved.

down in its growth and its progress? It is just simply because we haven't done our work. Every man must do his work.

In the Bible it is written so plainly, and aren't you glad for the plain things in the Scripture? This is the day of gobbledygook. Do you know what I mean by that? I don't know either, but I'll tell you what I think: Gobbledygook means more and more about less and less! All kinds of high sounding words and phrases and paragraphs and reams. Like a man in Arkansas one time who was on the city council of a little town. We just put out a bulletin with four pages of "governmenteze;" gobbledygook! And he said, "I could put this whole thing in one swarthy Anglo Saxon sentence: Don't throw your junk in the street!"

There was a pamphlet which came out of a government office (please forgive me) which had 29,811 words setting the price of cabbage! I'm so delighted that when I come to God's Book, I don't have to wade through reams and reams of gobbledygook and wonder what on earth they're talking about, like I wonder so many times when I pick up my insurance policy! And, God bless my insurance agent friends, but I do wish they would make it plainer! On the front page I'm promised so many beautiful things in big print. Then, that fine print which I have to put the glasses on for seems to take it all away from me!

Be that as it may, what I'm trying to say is that I just cry out for simplicity. Tell me what you mean; say what you mean. Tell me like it is, and when I come to the Book of God, I find that is what Jesus did. Not that there are no depths to plumb for the mature Christian. Sure, there is meat for the strong and advanced in the faith as well as milk for the babe, but the great basics are all in such simple language that a wayfaring man, though a fool, need not err therein.

"Come unto Me, all ye that labor and are heavy laden. I'll give you rest." Oh, hallelujah, that's a beauty!

"Believe on the Lord Jesus Christ and thou shalt be saved and thy house." That's a beauty.

"Bring all the tithes into the storehouse. Prove me now, herewith, saith the Lord and see if I'll not pour out a blessing upon thee." That's another beauty!

"The Lord is my Shepherd, I shall not want." That's another beauty!

Can I give you another beauty framed in gold? "Go ye into all the world and preach the Gospel to every creature." You do not have to wade through reams of gobbledygook to know what He meant; what He intended. He simply meant that we, the people of God to whom the Grace of God has come, should go into all the world and take the Good News to every creature; to go into every country and teach them all things whatsoever He has given us and commanded us, and to baptize them in the Name of the Father and the Son and the Holy Ghost, and then He said: (Are you listening?) "You go and I'll go with you. Lo, I am with you always, even unto the end of the world!"

It's time for me to cease, but I want to tell you that if I had time this morning, I could wax eloquent on the warranty that goes with this Operator's Manual for the Church. The Operator's Manual for the Church is the responsibility to get the Good News to everybody, everywhere, every place, every man, woman, and child! The miracle-born Church was sent forth with that Operator's Manual from heaven. And, there is a warranty that went with it; so much better than 12,000 miles or 12 months. "Lo, I am with you always, even to the end of the world."

If I had the time this morning, I would tell you about miracles that have taken place on the mission field. Of angelic hosts that have protected kids. You know that school you went to (speaking to Pastor Cummings), wasn't it the Rift Valley Academy? The marvelous thing that happened when God took care of those kids in the Mau-Mau days by circling the school with bright angels of flaming swords that put the Mau-Maus back and sent them into the woods. Glory be to God!

Oh, I could tell you of instance after instance where the words of a Perfect Gentleman, the Lord Jesus Christ, were fulfilled exactly like He said they would be. That leads me to say, "Come on, let's evangelize the world!"

It's a mission possible because Jesus told us to do it and He said, "What you lack, I'll supply." What a partnership! To go in with One Who knows everything and owns everything. Every bank. And, is too good to hurt anybody; too powerful to fail! Too wise to make a mistake. Can do anything and everything. To be invited into partnership with Him, you're right in putting that banner in this sanctuary:

"MISSION POSSIBLE!"

He said, "Go into all the world and I'll go with you." Let's give the Lord Jesus Christ the chance to show His magnificent Lordship and, **LET'S GO!**

REV. WESLEY R. HURST

Rev. Wesley R. Hurst began his missionary career in what was then Tanganyika (now Tanzania), East Africa, after pastoring churches in South Dakota and Montana. He and his wife, June, distinguished themselves as founders of the Tanganyika Bible Institute in Arusha which today is known as the Bible College of Tanzania. When serious illness forced Wes home to the United States, he served the Foreign Missions Department of the Assemblies of God as Home Secretary, directing public relations, publications, and promoting missions conventions in local churches. Later, he served the department 17 years as Field Director for the Far East. His territory extended from Burma (Myanmar) in the west to French Polynesia in the eastern South Pacific and from Korea in the north to New Zealand in the south. He was indefatigable as a missionary statesman, often gone for months at a time as he visited and encouraged more than 200 resident missionaries in 78 countries of the Asia/Pacific region. Wes Hurst was a dear friend who introduced me to ministry in Asia. He delivered the following message in Aurora on September 5, 1976.

— H. C.

Wes and June Hurst with Randy and Judy, as the family left for service in East Africa. Baby Brother Jahn, also now a missionary, joined them later!

4

"I AM A DEBTOR"

Rev. Wesley R. Hurst

Turn with me to the first chapter of Romans. I would like to read some verses from the heart of Paul as he writes to people he had never seen but loved. In the 11th verse he says, "I long to see you, that I may impart unto you some spiritual gift, to the end ye may be established." Then he says, in the 14th through 16th verses, most important truths with these very significant words:

"I am debtor both to the Greeks, and to the Barbarians; both to the wise, and to the unwise. So, as much as in me is, I am ready to preach the gospel to you that are at Rome also. For I am not ashamed of the gospel of Christ, for it is the power of God unto salvation to every one that believeth; to the Jew first, and also to the Greek."

Early this morning as I awakened, this phrase kept coming to me. Paul said, "I am a debtor." He could only be a debtor if he has received something, and Jesus said very clearly, "Freely ye have received; freely give." Paul, through the mercies of God, had received much and he considered himself thus a debtor. He owed the Greeks; he owed the Barbarians; and he felt a longing in his heart to deliver what he owed to the Romans. He wanted to meet them and he said, "I want to see you, because I want to give to you something spiritual; something that God has given to me." And he continued, "I am ready, so much as is in me, I am ready." It builds a nice outline: **I Am Ready; I Am Not Ashamed; I Am A Debtor!**

I AM READY!

All of us impacted by the Gospel of Jesus Christ are debtors. I'm a debtor of the Gospel; a debtor of the message; a debtor of the grace and mercies that God has given us.

As I stood in the hall this morning waiting to come into the sanctuary, my mind was not here. I stood thinking of people half a world away with whom I had worshipped not many Sundays ago in the land of Burma. As I went to church that morning in Rangoon, I went with a new feeling. I had been detained by immigration as a result of some foolish activities on the part of some independent "religious entrepreneurs" who had surreptitiously entered the country and involved themselves in illegal activities trying to distribute Bibles secretly on a military base. This individual was arrested and put in jail. As a result, a new law was declared so that as a visitor in Burma, I was not allowed to preach. Still, to this day, no one as a guest is allowed to minister in Burma anymore. For five, nearly six years, I've been able to go in and minister. But, no more.

As I entered the sanctuary, there were more people there than are here this morning. Ten years ago, our missionaries were obliged to leave Burma because of government laws and restrictions. No missionaries are allowed in Burma today. There is not one Catholic or one Protestant of any kind permitted. But the church has survived and grown. In Rangoon, less than 100 people were identified with the First Assembly ten years ago. Now, every Sunday there are at least 650 people that come to that church; and they have opened 12 satellites in the past ten years! They have many problems. Pastor Myo Chit was arrested one time for distributing tracts and preaching on the railroad platform because the crowd was so large. He knew his constitutional rights, and when the police arrested him he said, "What am I arrested for?" And, they said, "For preaching out here on this platform." He said, "You can't do that. I can propagate my faith anywhere. The constitution guarantees it and the President (Dictator) General Ne Win has pledged to keep and uphold the constitution. You can't arrest me for preaching." The policeman didn't know what to do with that and so they said, "Well, we are arresting you for obstructing the traffic out there on the platform." He said, "Give me two or three policemen to go out and control the crowd and let me go on with my constitutional rights." And so, instead of the people that arrested him, they were the ones that went out and guided the crowd so he could go on preaching and passing out tracts!! This is a socialist society that refused to allow me to preach just a few weeks ago.

The author presents a contribution check to Mr. Hurst to invest in the Rangoon Evangelistic Center during one of his many visits to Aurora.

As I sat in the head immigration man's office he said, "This man (as he pointed to Pastor Myo Chit) has religious freedom in this country. But," he said, "you do not; you're a foreigner." I said, "May I greet the people?" He replied, "No." When the pastor inquired, I was told I could not even stand on the church platform. So, my wife and I sat in the front seat as 650 people wept. They had come to hear some word from us as we had come to them. We spent a week in that country, followed by the Secret Service and those that were monitoring every movement we made. Even though I was not allowed to minister, those believers in Burma are **ready for anything! Ready, if need be, to give their life for the cause of Christ!**

I AM NOT ASHAMED!

As I go to Indonesia, I go to a country of 130 million people and I see our 40 missionaries who are there, and I realize how little they are in number in comparison to the task. Yet, I realize as I move throughout Indonesia, which is a country in itself that's 3,000 miles long and about 1,000 miles wide if you embrace the whole archipelago, that God is pouring out His Spirit. God is moving by His Spirit and great things are taking place; miracles, healings, people being saved miraculously. God is working by His Spirit and God is giving us opportunities beyond our imagination to share with those around this world the message of the Gospel of Jesus Christ. Much of this is accomplished because the believers in Indonesia, a Muslim country, are not ashamed to share their faith.

There are more doors open today than ever. A few years ago, in the missions office we were rejoicing over 62, 63, up to 65 countries in which we were laboring. Now we labor in 95 countries! I remember when we had 75 or 80 Bible schools; now we have 135. I remember when we had 2,000 students studying overseas; now we have more than 5,000 preparing for ministry. God is blessing; God is moving and there are national church bodies that are sending out missionaries today. **They are not ashamed!** The church in Fiji has four fulltime missionaries; the church in Japan is sending missionaries; the church in Korea has 12 fulltime missionaries. The church in the Philippines is sending missionaries; the church in Indonesia is preparing to send missionaries. We are seeing the "cross-webbing" of Gospel witness which is the result of the same thing that I read to you this morning. They have received and they are anxious to share; oblivious to danger, indebted, ready, not ashamed.

Many years ago, the missionaries went to Burma as a result of a unique experience. There were missionaries in China, and way up in the mountains there was a man from the Lisu tribe who went into one of the provinces, into one of the trade centers to buy salt, and he found Christ. He was filled with the Holy Spirit. He went back up into the mountains and began to share the message. It wasn't long until it began to spread among the Lisu tribe up in the mountains of upper Burma. Finally, these people called a missionary and the Morrisons went up, followed by the Staffords. Following them, the Ray Trasks. God blessed bountifully way up in the mountains. Today, there are 30,000. (Editor's note: as of 2006, 85,000.) They are surviving; they are carrying on in spite of repression, in spite of all that surrounds them. You know, it's wonderful to know that the Holy Spirit does not have to have a passport; doesn't have to have a visa; and He isn't required to go through immigration!

It was an odd feeling, as an American, to sit there in that church and want to preach with all my heart; to know that the people

Missionary James Hance, Rev. Wes Hurst, and the author at the South Pacific Missionary Retreat in 1979.

wanted to hear me preach and be forced to keep silent. The congregation sat there and wept. Pastor Myo Chit got up and preached about the coming of the Lord, and those people were more convinced than ever that Jesus is coming! God help us to be as convinced as they that He's coming. To be **Ready and Not Ashamed** of the Gospel!

Paul said he also was convinced and that he was "in debt." He was **Ready!** He was **Not Ashamed!** And, he considered himself to be in **Debt!**

I AM A DEBTOR

This is my feeling as I go back and forth into Burma and other places. The attitudes epitomize the feelings of the lost who have been redeemed! In many places: Japan, Korea, Singapore, Malaysia, Indonesia, the islands of the sea — places like Guadalcanal and Tongo and the New Hebrides (now Vanuatu) and New Caledonia — all of these places. The moment I see the people, I know names, places, churches, and I know people are struggling to stay alive. And, those who are lost and without God — I'm in debt to them! God gives us a sense of responsibility and a realization of what we really owe and how we can pay it.

There are young people in this room — God doesn't want just a $100 bill from you or a $1,000 faith promise — God wants you on this mission field. There are many parents — God not only wants your faith promise and faithful giving to missions — God wants a son or a daughter. God help this church to make the kind of offerings — not just the monthly offerings of money — the kind of offerings and prayer for people such as I have mentioned this morning. God help us to make the kind of offerings that will pay the debt we owe in response to the wonderful, gracious kindness of our Father in giving us Jesus. Paul said, **"I'm a Debtor!"**

In these countries I've mentioned, I realize how wonderful it is to live in America. How wonderful it is to have so much, but in having so much, we are debtors. We owe much, and we must give much. In having so much we have received from Him; from His hand, such liberties, such possibilities, such resources. We are in debt to God and to a lost world. We are in debt to people such as the Christians of Burma. God help us to pray for them. God help us to do what we can to help them. God help us to be aware of those in many lands who need this wonderful, wonderful message!!

Paul considered himself a **Debtor**. Every Christian is, and as we come to the table of the Lord this morning, we know that by the blood we are washed clean and all of that knowledge of faith moves through our beings. God help us to realize there are people who are groping in darkness. They have no eyes; they are blind, searching for the same kind of light that we take so for granted. God help us to **Pay our Debt!!**

REV. JAMES HANCE

We first met Jim Hance when I was honored to preach for the South Pacific Missionary Retreat held that year in Suva, Fiji. Jim was then serving as Area Director for the South Pacific region after devoting a number of years to ministry in American and Western Samoa, as well as Fiji. His ministry as Area Director included 13 island countries with pastoral oversight of 30 resident missionaries. We were privileged later to host Jim and Lou Hance in our missions crusade at Aurora.

Jim was a graduate of Central Bible College in 1956 and was ordained by the Michigan District of the Assemblies of God. He and Louella pastored churches in Wapato and Bellevue, Washington and in Coeur d'Alene, Idaho. They served as missionaries to the South Pacific from 1971 until 1986.

His untimely death shocked many of us. However, as the Scripture says, he still has something to say about the church and its responsibility to missions. The following message was preached by Jim Hance in Aurora on November 4, 1984.

— H. C.

The Hance family as they appeared when they entered foreign service.

5

"DO YOU KNOW WHAT TIME IT IS?"

Rev. James Hance

In Luke 19:41, the Gospel writer tells us that as Jesus beheld the city of Jerusalem, "He wept over it," bemoaning the fact that "thou knewest not the time of thy visitation."

And, in Romans 13:11–14, the Apostle declares, "Knowing the time, that now it is high time to awake out of sleep; for now is our salvation nearer than when we believed. The night is far spent, the day is at hand; let us therefore cast off the works of darkness, and let us put on the armor of light. Let us walk honestly, as in the day; not in rioting and drunkenness, not in chambering and wantonness, not in strife and envying. But put ye on the Lord Jesus Christ, and make not provision for the flesh, to fulfill the lusts thereof."

In light of these and other Scriptures, I feel in my heart a sense of the importance of the hour in which we live. We are in a time of destiny; a time peculiar in this generation of men, and I pray that tonight, as we share these words, the Holy Spirit will penetrate far deeper than my voice can go and that He will touch us with the realization of the hour in which we live.

Jesus came to His own people, and they received Him not. He walked the shores of their world; He walked the streets of their cities, and they refused to have Him. And Jesus wept as He looked over their capital city, realizing they had missed their opportunity. He saw what was coming, when everything would be turned upside down, and seeing this, He wept over the city because they knew not the hour of their visitation.

A few months ago while we were in Fiji, I remember hearing that the scientists of the world had advanced the minute hand of the "doomsday clock," from four to three minutes to twelve. They felt that because of the crisis in our world and the difficulty among nations, we are nearer the doomsday hour. I thought, "Is it possible that these scientific minds, as they evaluate the world scene, feel that we are close to the final hour and are publicizing it by advancing the minute hand on their clock?"

I believe that if anybody ought to know the hour in which we live it is the Church of Jesus Christ. We need to realize the time and be awake to the hour in which we live. The biggest business in our world today is the manufacturing and sale of arms. Every nation is buying and stockpiling weapons. It seems as though they are preparing for Armageddon; for a showdown of nations. I believe we are in a dangerous hour; the non-religious people are talking about it, and the Church cannot afford to be asleep. The Church cannot afford to be indifferent to the conditions of our world. These are the last days and the Church must be awakened. We must be on full alert. Romans 13 says the night is far spent and that sin is about to come to maturity. Mankind can only get so evil and so wicked. There is a limit to where man can go in his degeneration and straying from God.

In the parable of the tares, when the servants asked about the weeds growing with the wheat, "Should we go out and pull them up?" Jesus replied, "Let both grow until the harvest. Let them ripen together, and in the time of harvest, it will be easy to separate the tares from the wheat. I believe both crops are ripening.

The Church is moving into God and becoming more mature in faith at the same time the world is degenerating and turning away from God; evil is becoming more extreme and the crop is ripening. I don't know how much further we can go, but I think we are near that time when the judgment and wrath of God is going to be poured out upon this world!

When one is out of the country for awhile and comes back periodically to America, you can see the definite changes that have taken place. You can remember how it was when you left and come back where little is the same. The changes are obvious to us whereas, living in America, things happen so gradually that you may not readily notice. We came back in August of this year, and frankly, I'm concerned about our nation. I am praying for God to help America. One area of concern is this matter of abortion. God in heaven is surely troubled by the direction our nation has gone. Listening to the news the other day, I heard the announcer say

Jim and Lou Hance in a South Pacific setting, Area Directors for a vast Region.

that in California at an abortion clinic, they were trying to decide what to do with 15,000 fetuses. They had them in formaldehyde barrels and they were going to take them out and bury them. Pro-abortionists cried, "No, if you bury them, you are acknowledging that they are human!" Others said they should just take them to the city dump! My heart breaks when I realize what is happening in our country. We need to be disturbed. Do you know the fine for destroying the egg of an eagle? It's a fine of $5,000 to destroy the egg of our national bird, but it's legal to destroy a human fetus.

I heard recently that it is impossible for a young girl to go in and have her ears pierced without the permission of her parents, but she can go and have an abortion without telling them! Now, something is bad wrong! Last year in America, 1.6 million abortions! May God help us — the night is far spent!

I'm concerned about homosexuality. Gradually, the public opinion and attitudes have changed. I come home now and hear people on television, such as the "pastor" of a homosexual church! I couldn't believe it! This pastor, an avowed homosexual, says that 80% of his congregation is homosexual and he claims that the passages in Romans about this behavior are being "misinterpreted!" What nonsense! God has been clear in His Word; He has stated as plain as He can, and yet people seem not to care about what God says. This behavior triggers the wrath of God!

I understand that in Britain now in the public schools, they bring in homosexuals to explain the various lifestyles so that the boys and girls can choose whichever they want! Ladies and gentlemen, the night is far spent!

I don't want to take all of my time speaking of the "night" because I have something better to say to you, but I do feel that we need to realize we haven't much time. Even in our paradise islands in the South Pacific, the invasion of darkness is strong. In Western Samoa, we now lead the world in suicides. In a beautiful place, where you think everything is idealic, the clash of cultures and the problems of sin are so real that young people cannot cope, so they drink weed killer! This, friends, is their favorite way to go! It takes about two weeks to die as this poison eats their vital organs and they die an agonizing, tormenting death. American Samoa has the third highest beer consumption in the world, only topped by Germany and Australia! Fiji has the highest number of prison inmates per capita. So there is no place in the world which has escaped the darkness covering our world. The night is far spent!

But, **I have good news for you!** The rest of the verse says, "the day is at hand!" We believers are not of the night; we're not going down with the ship! We're going up with the King when He comes, and I believe He is coming soon! We are living near the end of this age. Jesus is soon to come, and He has a great and glorious future planned! The last chapter of this world's history is going to be glorious; Jerusalem will be the capital and the righteous government of Jesus Christ will prevail over this world. A King is coming who is going to change things, and I say "Hallelujah!"

I'm convinced that the quicker we get the job done, it's that much sooner the King is coming. He said, "This Gospel of the Kingdom shall be preached in all the world as a witness to all nations, and then shall the end come!" So, let's get on with it! Let's get the job done so that we can get out of here! Hallelujah! Amen!

So, you see, when we talk missions and about supporting the work of God overseas, we're talking about hastening the Day of the Lord. All the prophets saw it coming. May God help us to see it.

One of the things promised about the last days is, "I will pour out my Spirit upon all flesh." Today, we are in a time of spiritual revival and it is a sign to us that these are the last days.

I was raised in a Pentecostal preacher's home. In those days, there was a stigma attached to being Spirit-filled people. When we came back from Africa, my father's health was poor and he took a small church down by the Ohio River in Martin's Ferry. The building was run down, the high water mark for the last flood was a foot from the ceiling, there was an old pot-bellied stove in the middle, and just a few believers. As a kid, I was embarrassed to go to the little church. But, in my lifetime, the Spirit-filled fellowships have moved from down by the railroad tracks, down by the river, to the best neighborhoods in town! The moving of the Spirit is "in" today; it has touched the highest levels of society! This is a sign to me that God is fulfilling His Word! He has poured out His Spirit as He said. It's happening all over the world. Now, the reason for the outpouring of the Spirit is to equip us for the task; to enable us to get on with it and do the work He has commissioned us to do!

I'm convinced that this is the greatest hour for the Church. This last day, eleven o'clock harvest is going to be the greatest time of ingathering we've ever seen, and the reports I get from around the world from other missionaries is that it's happening all over. Let me share some reports from the field to let you know what is happening:

In Fiji we are seeing revival. For about the last 20 years the work in Fiji has really blossomed from just four or five churches to over 100, some of them reaching thousands. At the present time, we have no building in Fiji that can house church conventions or great meetings. This move of God is touching other denominations!

A few years ago, when I was here, I mentioned the revival in the **Marshall Islands** and how some islands are almost totally evangelized. Our fellowship includes over 15% of the population, not even counting other evangelical groups! New churches are being opened and young people are being trained to reach their area. At the beginning of one of our conventions, a young man and his wife were converted; he is now the senator representing the island of Bikini. Just a few days ago after a protracted meeting in the Marshalls, they baptized 265 people in one service!!

Tahiti, let me talk about that. I am so thrilled with the response of this Aurora church in helping us in the Tahiti project. This has real Biblical significance because it is reaching a part of the world that is truly "the uttermost parts!" The last thing Jesus said before returning to the Father was that His followers were to take the Gospel to "Jerusalem, Judea, Samaria, and the uttermost part of the earth." The "uttermost" is about 800 miles south and east of Tahiti; an island called Rapa. This is literally the uttermost so, in actuality, Jesus said we are not to stop until we get to Rapa! Take the Gospel all the way. Now, just two weeks ago, we dedicated the new building in Tahiti which you have helped us build and this will be the lighthouse to reach French Polynesia and all the way to Rapa! What a great prospect that soon our Lord will say, "All right church, you've got the job done!"

Last year, while in Tahiti, I was looking for land for this building. We had teams ready to come, money was set aside for the project, but we needed land to put the building on. Our missionaries had been looking for about four months and could not find a thing. The properties in the area were selling for $300,000–$400,000 for just small lots, which were totally inadequate. So, I was looking and it was discouraging. About a week before we were to leave, I heard of this property we now have. I looked at it and decided this was the one we wanted, so I called Brother Hurst (Field Director for Asia) and he gave the go ahead. I had him send $20,000 to put down, but you know it's a difficult thing to stand up there on a hillside, all by yourself and look at a property that's going to cost $130,000 and make the decision all by yourself. I was praying that God would please direct me. So, I took my wife up there to look at it for encouragement. It was a rainy day, and as we stood there in the brush on that piece of property, she said, "You want to buy THIS?"

While we were talking to the lawyer, the phone rang and the Mormon Church called to offer them $160,000 for the property! I said, "Wait a minute. We are first in line and we're going to take it for $130,000!" So, we got the property.

Shortly after, we were out surveying, looking over the property and getting some ideas of how to fit the construction in, some men came out who know real estate and said, "This property is worth $1 million!" Obviously, we have an ideal property which God has given us and now, we have a building on the property seating 400 people. God is moving by His Spirit!

Some of you are acquainted with Randy and Renee' Carlson, two young people this church supports. They are in **Palau.** I've been praying for years that God would open this nation; that He would send someone to plant the Church of Jesus Christ on this lonely island. Randy and Renee' went in, without any congregation, without any openings at all, just going absolutely fresh to start a church. The first thing another denominational missionary told Randy was "You cannot get land in this country. We have tried. We have looked. We've been here three years. We can't get land for anything!"

Randy said, "Well, we'll just trust God and pray." Well, God gave him favor with the governor of the state of Arrai. Randy said, "You know, governor, we need to get land to build a house and to build a church." The governor said, "Well, let me show you some land I have." He took him around and Randy said, "How about this one?" It had been bulldozed, leveled, a driveway cut, right on a hilltop with a fantastic view between two villages. The governor said, "Well, my son was planning to build on this property, but he's changed his mind! I'll tell you what I'll do, Reverend. I'll let you have this piece of land, a twenty-five year lease with right of renewal and how about $120 a year lease payment?"

Fantastic! Hallelujah! That's how God works; in a place where you can't get land, you can't buy land, you can't lease land, God let's you know He wants to do something in that little country!! They got a little tent and started having their first meetings. The first night they put up the tent, it rained torrential island-style rain! They had 25 people there. When Randy gave the altar call, 12 of these people got saved right in a rainstorm!

Recently, I called the Miami Tent Company and ordered three tents which a church in Tacoma is going to help us buy for three different island countries. While I was talking with them, they said, "Oh, we got a call from Reverend Carlson in Palau and he's ordered a center section for his tent. He's having such crowds that he needs another addition in his tent to accommodate them. The day is at hand; believe me, it's harvest time!

One of the main thrusts we have in the islands is Bible schools. We believe we can never touch the 4,000 islands by sending missionaries only, but the key is to train national people and send them out. I am so blessed with the quality of national brethren we have in the islands. Fine men who love God. We then put these men into teaching situations to teach young people and send them out. We have six such Bible schools in the island countries. The largest is in Fiji, which has about 70 students. The other five are vernacular schools in the different island countries, and from these schools is going a real army of young people out to preach the Gospel. In Guadalcanal, where the Marines first came ashore on Red Beach in World War II, we have four acres and a Bible school. Young people are going out from there in a spiritual invasion to touch all of the **Solomon Islands**. I'm excited about our schools; I'm excited about the response we are getting.

In the Bible school in **Samoa**, we are getting 95% of the graduates going into fulltime Gospel work. We are thrilled and we are praying that God will just continue to raise up a mighty army.

I believe with all my heart that this is our last day to reach the world. If you ever planned to pray, pray now. If you've ever planned to give to reach our world, give now. If you've ever planned to dedicate your life and sell out to God, do it now, because it's harvest time! The night is far spent; the day is at hand, and it is time for us to do all we can to see our world evangelized.

REV. KENNETH GODBEY

The camera was rolling as the interview with Kenneth and Geraldine Godbey got underway. I was transfixed once again by his hands; having heard the story, I wanted my audience to know the reason for the obvious scars. So, I asked the Godbey's to share. Mr. Godbey had suffered severe burns over 90% of his body when a kerosene powered appliance at the mission station had exploded. He rushed into the room, picked up the burning appliance and carried it out, saving the entire building but at the risk of himself. Flown home for treatment, his family and friends despaired for his life. But, God restored him to health with only the gnarled and scarred hands as a vivid reminder that, in this, Ken Godbey joined the Apostle Paul: "I bear in my body the marks of the Lord Jesus." (Galatians 6:17) It's a picture forever imprinted in my mind!

Kenneth and Geraldine Godbey were pioneer missionaries to Nigeria, arriving in West Africa after an arduous ocean journey during World War II, with their liner dodging German U-boat attacks on the high seas. Conditions forced long separations from their young son, Keith, and with little sister Donna, born in Africa. The situation was primitive. But, together with other missionaries, a beachhead was established which today results in a Nigerian fellowship of over two million baptized members. The ultimate tribute to their identity with the Incarnate Deity, who gave the original missions command and was Himself the first missionary, was a poignant moment as they approached retirement when Nigerian leaders said to Kenneth Godbey: "You are now **one of us!**" These

African leaders no longer considered them "American preachers;" they were truly Nigerian!

That, friends, is why I believe that these missionary heroes, though now with Jesus, "still speak!" This message, which illustrates the total commitment of the career missionary to learn the language, adopt the customs, and become "one" with the national Christians in the country of ones' calling, was preached in Aurora on January 4, 1976.

— H. C.

Kenneth and Geraldine Godbey served as missionaries to Nigeria for four decades.

6

"YOU ARE NOW ONE OF US"

Rev. Kenneth Godbey

It's been a long time since we were face-to-face with you. Your pastor has spoken about a team and it is. It takes a team to carry through with the responsibility that the Lord has given to His Church. It's not accomplished by one, two, or three individuals; it's an effort put forth by every child of God, adding their abilities, talents, and the anointing of the Spirit of God upon their lives, all contributing together in order that this commission given to the Church by our great Commander-in-Chief be accomplished.

The other day I heard a statement which I pondered over many hours. The man who spoke these words, as far as I know, is not a believer; he was speaking in the secular realm, but, he said — "Oh, the emptiness of an **existence without commitment!**" Think it over. The world sees the necessity of setting a goal, working toward that goal, and with this there must be commitment. The same truth holds for the Christian.

God has not put us here by accident. God has designed a purpose in and through every one of us. Who are we? Where are we going? What's out there ahead? What are we eventually reaching for? God has something for us to do; He has a purpose for our lives before we are translated and make heaven our home.

There is a story of a man coming into a strange city, seeking an address which he thinks he can find. I've done this over and over.

I don't know what it is about male ego, but we don't want to admit we don't know where we're going. My wife will say, "What's the address?" I'll answer vaguely, "It's so and so." She'll say, "Do you know where you're going?" I'll reply that I do, and here we go, up one street and down another, back to the main street of the town, finally ending up in frustration. She'll reach over and tap me on the arm, "Honey, why don't you stop and ask?"

This is what this man was doing; trying to find this address. He couldn't find it; and finally in complete frustration he comes back to the main thoroughfare, stops at a light and a vehicle in front of him has a bumper sticker on it: "Don't follow me, I'm lost too!"

How true of many Christians. Friends, God has not put us here to take pot shots at the heavens and hope that somehow our labors and our substance will eventually, some way accomplish what God has in mind.

God has a purpose. God has a goal for you. You say, "What's this got to do with missions?" It's got everything to do with missions. Whether you live in America, Africa, Latin America, or some other nation of the world, people rarely read a Bible. Instead, they read our lives; and if your life and mine is to be effective for the purpose for which God has placed us here, then He expects unreserved commitment of our lives, our resources, and all that we ever hope to be.

My text is in John 17, verses one and two, the actual words of Jesus: "Father, the hour is come. Glorify Thy Son that Thy Son also may glorify Thee. As thou hast given Him power over all flesh that He should give eternal life to as many as Thou has given Him and, this is life eternal...." What a beautiful, simple definition of salvation!

"I have glorified Thee on the earth. I have finished the work which Thou gavest Me to do, and now, oh Father, glorify Thou Me with thine Own Self with the glory which I had with Thee before the world was. I have manifested Thy Name unto the men which Thou gavest Me out of the world." I want you to note these words: "I have manifested, I have revealed, I have made known." Another version says, "I have manifested Your Name, I have revealed Your very Self, Your real Self to the people whom Thou has given Me."

This is the **First Purpose for which Christ came: to reveal to a lost world what the Heavenly Father was like. The Second Purpose is simple: to complete the redemption of lost humanity.**

NOTE THE ORDER: Revealing what the Father was like and secondly, giving them the Words the Father had given to Him to bring redemption.

You and I are in this world, young or old, grandma or grandpa, for the purpose of showing the world what God the Father is like. We cannot add to His glory. God has all glory. However, we as created beings, because of the indwelling Christ in us, can and will glorify Him before the world.

Now, there has to be a beginning; where does it all start? Go back to the beginning in Genesis 1:26–27. Here God tells us that man was created in the Divine image. Have you ever questioned as to what that image involved? Some time ago, I believe God gave me at least a portion of the answer. Did being "created in His image" mean that man was created holy as God is holy? I can't accept that and I'll tell you why: If man was created in the holiness of God, and then man fell, it would infer that it's possible for God to fall and that cannot be.

What does the "image of God" mean? What was it in God that God imparted to man? Remember this: God is a person. He's a personality; He has a mind; He's omniscient; He knows all things from the beginning to the end; He has a seat of emotions; He has a heart; He loves, He hates. He hates sin; He grieves; He experiences sorrow; and God has a Will — a Sovereign Will, and at least in a measure, God imparted these ingredients of personality to man. You are a personality; I'm a personality. God has given each of us a mind with which to comprehend and understand the things of God, but natural man in his fallen condition cannot comprehend the things of God. It's impossible. The Scripture tells us that the natural mind "receiveth not the things of God."

God imparted to man a seat of emotions, a heart originally intended to be able to reciprocate the love that God bestowed upon man. And, God gave man a will with which to decide his own future and whether or not he would obey God. You will remember that it was in the realm of that will that man disobeyed God and fell from grace, and as a result, sin and death passed upon all humanity. You find that picture in Romans chapter one. A dark picture. Man's mind was darkened; his heart was debauched and degraded, and his will could not and would not obey God. That is the condition that you find man apart from Jesus Christ.

I ask you the question: How can such a creature, no matter what they do or how they involve themselves, how can that creature glorify God? It's not possible.

The answer comes in the writings of Paul when he said, "If any man be in Christ Jesus, he is a new creation; old things are passed away, behold all things are become new." This is the new beginning. Mankind has been created anew. The Spirit of God actually imparts — creates in the repentant sinner — a new mind which is able to comprehend and understand the things of God; a heart that is able to reciprocate the love of God, and a will that wants to obey Him.

Man can only glorify God — show the world what God is like — when, in Christ Jesus, he lives a life in conformity to the Person of Jesus Christ. Don't misunderstand me. I'm not saying there is one of us absolutely perfect, but I am saying that to the degree you submit to God and the Holy Spirit in your life — allow the Holy Spirit to accomplish His purpose — only then will men and women see Jesus Christ. And when they see Jesus, He reveals what God is like.

Jesus said, "If I be lifted up, I will draw all men unto me." How is He lifted up? By seeing Jesus at work in your life and mine.

Kenneth and Geraldine Godbey as they neared retirement.

Jesus said, "You shall receive power after that the Holy Ghost has come upon you and you shall be witnesses." As Pentecostal people, under the anointing of the Holy Spirit, we should be witnesses.

There is something a little deeper that I think we should consider right here that God spoke to me this last term on the field. I was snowed under with responsibilities. I was tired and weary. My mind was exhausted, and when this happens to me, there is a tendency to become irritable and to not allow the Spirit of God to lead and direct my life. One day following family worship, which is a custom in our home, I wasn't satisfied, so I went into a bedroom in the mission station and shut the door. I made up my mind I was going to stay there until I got some answers. After I had talked and talked to God and prayed and prayed and wept before Him. (You know, God will let you do that just as long as you want to do it. He'll sit by very patiently and listen to everything you have to say, and when you are finished, then the still small voice speaks.) He said to me, "My son, I'm not so interested in how great things are and how many things you do for me or think you're doing for Me. **I am vitally concerned with what you are!**

My knees were not low enough. Flat on my face before God, I poured out my heart to Him. I want to tell you friends, if there is any one thing that hinders the missionary effort at home and abroad, it's individuals who are not yielded to be what God wants them to be.

The national Christians on a mission field, in a matter of three to six months will have a name for every one of the missionaries. They don't tell the missionary what that name is. And, oh, when I look back at the mistakes I've made, I think, "Dear Lord, how did these dear brethren ever have patience to put up with my nonsense?" But they do, and they love the missionaries.

We're not perfect yet; but God is working on it if we'll permit Him to do so, and it's for the purpose that this sin-darkened world in chaos might see Jesus Christ. This is missions. It's the very basis, the foundation of missions. And, as God works His purpose, there are times when we do not understand what He is doing. But, there are certainly truths which are obvious:

1. God makes no mistakes.
2. There is nothing that happens to the child of God but what first our Heavenly Father permits it.
3. If God permits it to happen, He has done it for our good.

His Word says plainly, "All things work together for good to them that love God, to them who are called according to His purpose."

Why some of these things happen, we sometimes question. August 25, 1971, we were sitting at lunch in one of our lady missionary's home at the Bible School compound at Agocha. A kerosene refrigerator began to smoke and act up. The wick was stuck and couldn't be turned down. In trying to remedy the situation, I tried to take the tank out. In the course of trying, the tank exploded and I was covered with burning kerosene from head to foot. All of my clothes burned off. I was left in a dying condition standing on my feet, my skin, my flesh hanging like Spanish moss from a tree. The fluids were running out of my body excessively. I knew I was facing death. I couldn't see my face, but my wife could, and she said it was a horrible sight. The flesh rolled up over my nose. By all rights, I should be so deformed that it wouldn't be comfortable to go out in public without a mask on. You would probably not want to sit in your seats and look at me. (Maybe you don't want to anyway!!) Yet, not a mark on my face is left from that terrible ordeal. Sixty to seventy percent of my body burned with second and third degree burns, laying in a little Catholic maternity hospital for two nights and days with no help except putting fluids back in my body through a needle inserted in a vein in my foot.

Friends were finally able to get a small missions plane from a sister mission to fly in on a football field and pick up my wife and me. They delivered me to Jos, Nigeria, where there was a hospital and competent doctor. I lay there, hovering between life and death for several weeks. One of our single lady missionaries, a registered nurse, Doris Geiger, worked with my wife, both of them 24 hours a day, taking care of me. I couldn't even scratch my nose!

Then, in the wee hours of one morning (I don't remember any of this), I was completely unconscious. Doris said I suddenly sat up in the hospital bed and began singing the chorus — "He touched me, oh He touched me. And, oh the joy that floods my soul!*" She said I sang it through, never missing a note, a word, or a beat; sang it perfectly, my voice absolutely clear. I lay back down on that hospital bed, and from that moment, I began to mend!

When we finally arrived back in the states, we visited Central Assembly in Wichita, Kansas. Brother Edwin Lack, pastor at the time, said, "I want to tell you something. When we heard what had happened to you, I told my people to pray." One of the dear, elderly ladies who had passed away just a few weeks

---

*HE TOUCHED ME/William J. Gaither/© 1964 Gaither Music Company (ASCAP)/All rights controlled by Gaither Copyright Management. Used by permission.

before we visited, called the pastor one morning and said, "Pastor, Brother Godbey is going to be all right. God has undertaken for him!"

Somebody spent time enough to get hold of God and I'm here tonight because people prayed! I could literally feel the prayers of God's people as if it were a mattress under me. When you face death, as I did, it's a wonderful comfort to know where you are going and Who you are going to meet!

Don't be discouraged when the circumstances of life lay you flat on your back or something happens in your life or that of your family you don't understand. Pray, seek God's face and don't give up. God sometimes permits things to happen to us to bring us to the place where He can use us. Where we are pliable enough to surrender.

Where are you tonight? Have you made a complete commitment? The end makes it all worthwhile. Listen to these words: "When Christ, Who is our life shall appear, then shall you also appear with Him in glory." It's referring to our future. Glorified together with Christ. The trials of life gone. The imperfections in your life — gone. Complete in Christ and presented to the Father to hear Him say, "Well done, good and faithful servant!"

Friends, we're in this together. It isn't just your missionaries. This is God's work; we are a team. We are working together for the Kingdom of God, whether it's in Aurora, Colorado or in Africa!

Watched a football game lately? I wonder how far they would get if every man did his own thing? Not very far, I'm afraid. I know what I'd do if one of those 250 pound tackles headed for me; I'd run the other way!

But, this is a team effort. And, no Christian is going to be permitted to sit complacently by and say that everything is fine and coast into the Kingdom. We are to live so that those who need Christ will see Him at work in our lives. They may not read the Bible, but they will see something in us that will turn them to the Lord.

Just before we left Africa, I sat for the last time as one of the Executive Committee of the leadership in Nigeria. The leader, Brother Gabriel Oyakolubi, said, "Brother Godbey, I want you to know something before you go home. **You are now one of us!"**

I have never had a higher compliment paid to me in all my life. As far as they were concerned, I was thinking black, I was a black man. It meant the world to me. Not because I was perfect, but that I had achieved identity. They saw Jesus in my life and He related to them, not just to Americans.

A number of years ago, I had the privilege of standing before a group of 15 elderly men, representatives of their villages in that part of Africa. Wizened, wrinkled of skin, gray-haired men, they were the "law" of their villages. They had gathered to hear what the white man had to say before granting him permission to talk to the peoples of their villages. I brought them a very simple message, based upon Exodus and the Ten Commandments. I concluded by saying that God, in Christ Jesus, had made it possible for us to keep those Commandments. When I concluded, one elderly, stooped old man with gray hair, stood to his feet. He said, "I would like to speak. Sir, if what you have told us from God's Book is true, then we are guilty of sinning against God. I would like to know why we weren't told many years ago?"

Pastor Cummings, interviewing the Godbey's shortly before Ken's homegoing, showing the audience the scars on his hands, received in a terrible fire in Africa.

To Look At His Hands*
A Tribute to Missionary
Kenneth Godbey

Missionary Kenneth Godbey comes from an era of missionary service described many times by my friend Morris Williams as "unqualified commitment."

You could sense it in his heart, synchronized with the great heartbeat of God in concern over the lost, from the moment he was saved.

You could see it in his unquestioning submission to his brethren, when they said he was needed in Nigeria, and the subsequent willingness to endure hardship, such as leaving a little son when

*Eulogy composed for the funeral of Missionary Ken Godbey

the government would not grant children visas, and then risk the dangers of enemy submarines on the high seas during World War II, as well as the primitive conditions under which the Godbey's labored.

But most of all, you could see it in his hands. Those hands, horribly scarred when he suffered terrible burns carrying an exploding appliance out of the mission's compound, no doubt saving the lives of other missionaries and nationals by his heroism, and in the process shortening his illustrious missions career.

A few months ago, in an interview with Brother and Sister Godbey, I held those hands for a moment, and asked him, "If you had it to do over, would you?" Without hesitation, he said, "I'd go in a minute!" I was reminded of what Luke said concerning our risen Lord, when he wrote, "He showed them His hands…" The disciples knew!

To look at the hands of Ken Godbey was to know…to know what unqualified commitment is.

What a comfort now to know that the nail-scarred hands have received the labor-scarred hands of Kenneth Godbey, and granted him new ones!

Howard Cummings

REV. MORRIS WILLIAMS

Rev. Morris Williams, with his wife, Macey, served as a missionary to Africa from 1946 to 1985. His ministry was primarily in what is known today as Malawi (then Nyasaland) as well as in South Africa. The concluding 15 years of his service to Africa were as Field Director of the entire Continent for his denomination. Morrie, as we knew him, entered North Central Bible Institute (now North Central University) as an All-American high school football star from North Dakota, having passed up an athletic scholarship to a major university to follow the Lord's calling. He and Macey pastored a church in Moville, Iowa before entering foreign service. He also served as the Youth Director for the Iowa District (then known as the North Central District) of the Assemblies of God.

It was Morris Williams who helped some of us understand the depth of meaning in the term — "unqualified commitment." His commitment to Jesus Christ was just that, and it serves effectively as a backdrop for the following message, preached in Aurora on November 6, 1977.

— H. C.

The Morris Williams family on their first missionary prayer card, listing their assignment as Nyasaland, British East Africa. (Now Malawi)

7

"THE MAN AND THE WOMAN GOD USES"

Rev. Morris Williams

As I think back on my childhood, having come out of a North Dakota home during the depression where $5 was big money, I remember peddling milk in our hometown of Egland, North Dakota, a "big city" of 333 people. We sold milk for six cents a quart, and we never had milk on our own table because we had to sell all the milk in order to get enough money to live on. I would go around town shouting, "Williams Dairy at your service: pasteurized, sterilized, deodorized, balkanized!"

My parents were never grumblers and I didn't know that we went through hard times. I thank God for parents like that. But, we did grow up in a conservative era. I never dreamed that God would put me into a ministry like this.

I think of this school we are going to have in East Africa now that Ethiopia is closed for a time. I use the word "closed" in the same way we used it in referring to China for our American missionaries. But, we're going to have a school in East Africa which will cost about a quarter of a million dollars! And, we're going to go into Mombasa, Kenya. Some of you have heard of Morris Plotts; he was in a service and he mentioned he wanted to help with the Mombasa project. We hadn't even set a figure yet, but as he spoke of the project, somebody in the audience said, "I want to take that myself and I have $150,000!" Boom! Just like that. All taken care of. Just overwhelming!

You move into a realm when you work with God of the impossible and it's a thrilling thing. It's rather awesome, of course, to be a steward of these things. I think about the printing press we've just finished the building for in Accra, Ghana, which serves 10 countries in Africa. I don't know how it ever came in, but we have raised and paid for a $135,000 building! It is just amazing what God can do when He can find people who are willing to believe and work with Him. And tonight, I want to talk about the man and the woman that God uses, because God's eye is looking over believers to find people that He can use in a special way.

I think of the words of Brother Hogan (J. Philip Hogan) so many times as we interview new missionary candidates. As he talks to them, once in a while we get some person you just sense the tremendous potential in a life, and I can hear him say, "Brother and Sister, we sit here year after year praying that in Thailand (or some other country) God will find a man or a woman who will rise above the ordinary strata of people in faith and in ministry and will somehow bring awakening to that country!"

I believe that tonight God is looking right here for men and women He can use, because the truth is there are many Christians in the world, but so many of them God can't use because they won't make the type of consecration necessary. Tonight, I want to talk about the kind of person that God uses. I hope this church can be a church that is specially used. There are churches I believe God will use in this last day in a special way and raise them up to become missionary-minded to fit a real need in the world. You can be one of those churches!

How many of you brought your imagination along tonight? Now, I'm going to be a little uninhibited tonight. You'll excuse me, but we're all a little tired. We've watched football games this weekend; we've listened to preachers preach, and I don't want anyone to go to sleep on me as I talk. I'm going to use as my text Numbers 6, and I hope as you listen, you'll hold that Faith Promise in your hand and keep saying — "God, talk to me and help me to be that special person who will rise above the ordinary; who'll rise above the norm of Christian behavior, and that I will be used in a special way to meet a need."

This is the passage of scripture that talks about the Nazarite. A Nazarite was an Israelite who was specially selected by God to do a particular work of deliverance. Now, remember there were lots of Israelites, but not all Israelites were Nazarites. Conversely, there are many Christians whom God can never use because they will not make the commitment necessary to be specially used of God. So, the eye of God is roving on us tonight looking for a young man or woman who'll say, "Yes, I'll consecrate above the norm. I'll do more. I'm ready to move." Anybody who will say, "I'll serve, I'll teach, I'll give myself, I'll give my time." Somebody who refuses to settle for the norm of ordinary Christian behavior and says, "Lord, I'm ready to rise above it that I might be used of God."

It says in the 6th chapter of Numbers, the first and second verse, "The Lord spake unto Moses saying, 'speak unto the children of Israel, and say unto them, when either man or woman shall separate themselves; (if you will volunteer) to vow the vow of a Nazarite.'" And, He says it again, "To separate themselves unto the Lord." Then, God gives three things that are necessary for a person who wants to be used of God.

Are you ready now to follow me? Okay!

The first requirement for the one who would be used of God is in verse 3: "He shall separate himself from wine and strong drink and shall drink no vinegar of wine, or vinegar of strong drink, neither shall he drink any liquor of grapes nor moist grapes or dried. All the days of his separation shall he eat nothing that is made of the vine tree, from the kernels even to the husk."

How many believe that we should refrain from wine if we are going to be used by God? Let me see your hand. Raise them high — let me see them! Okay, the man or the woman whom God would use must refrain from wine. So, the first requirement is no wine. Say it — "NO WINE!" Say it again, "no wine!"

Okay, let's get the second one. Verse 5: "All the days of the vow of his separation there shall no razor come upon his head." You're not to cut your hair anymore. How many agree? Hey, I got my young people with me! What's the matter with you parents? You kind of left me on that one, but it's in the Bible! No wine, and the second one is no razor. Let's say it — "NO WINE, NO RAZOR!" Say it again, "no wine, no razor!" You say, "Brother, what are you talking about?" Let's keep going; this is the Scripture.

Verse 6 is the third requirement: "All the days that he separates himself unto the Lord he shall come at no dead body." No more funerals! How many agree? You've left me completely now, but that's what the Bible says. The man or the woman that God would use: no wine, no razor, no dead body! Let's say it together — "NO WINE, NO RAZOR, NO DEAD BODY!" They're awake now!

All right, I've done this deliberately. You know this and I'm not here to advocate we all become social dropouts, but usually when you find a passage like this, you will find some spiritual application which we can take to ourselves and that is what I'm going to do now. I'm going to find a spiritual application for no wine, no razor, no dead body, and out of this I think I can suggest the three things that are required of those who would rise above the norm. Now remember, this is not a separation of believers from unbelievers. This is a separation of certain believers from other believers who are not willing to make the commitment. Remember that. God is asking for special people who will rise above the norm to the place where they can be used of God. Now, let's get to our three points.

SELF-DENIAL

No wine. What would that stand for? Well, why does a man drink? To please his wife? To please his children? He uses wine for one reason only and that is to please himself; his flesh. And there is your point. The man or the woman whom God would use must not please himself. Self-denial is the first requisite for the man or the woman that God would use. Self-denial. Let's say it: "Self-denial!" We live in a country of the right of the individual; where we have it preached at us in the newspaper and through the media and in the school — the right of the individual to do his thing. And, if he thinks it is right, it is all right because he thinks it's right! We're taught not to deny ourselves. But, the man or the woman who would rise above the norm of ordinary Christians whom God can really use must come to the place where they say, "Lord, I will deny myself and I'll go without. I'll do whatever is necessary, what You want done to bring deliverance to the people of this world."

SEPARATION

Now, the second thing. I told you that you would have to use your imagination tonight because this is "Williams' Translation" of this Scripture. No wine — no razor. Now, you have a very handsome pastor, but let's use our imagination. Let's suppose that Pastor Cummings had not cut his hair for the last 16 years. He would be a beautiful sight! His hair would be way back down here, and when he went out on the streets of Aurora, do you think he'd attract any attention? I think he would, whether favorable or unfavorable. I rather think that a lot of people would look back that way and say "hum." Wouldn't they? He'd be a marked man. He would be a man who was not like the normal, everybody else. He would be different and his difference would sometimes cause people to laugh at him and he would be the butt of many a joke.

All right, I come to my point. If we are going to be willing to be used of God, we've got to be willing to be different! We live in a world of conformity where peer pressure says we've got to be like everybody around us and we can't stand to be different. It's humiliating if skirts are worn to here, to wear skirts down to here! You've got to conform, and I use a ridiculous illustration because that's not the important thing. But, there are many things that seem important where we're conforming when we shouldn't conform and it's very important to us parents. I got at the young people; I used something that young people are criticized for — hair and all of this business. But, what about the kind of car you drive, the house you live in? You've got to keep up with the (are there any Jones' here?). You've got to keep up with you-know! We live in a world of conformity, and because we're bound to be like everybody else, God can't use the "normal" (quote, unquote) Christian, He's looking around for people who will say, "Lord, I don't care what people think. The only thing I care about is doing Your will and seeing Your job done. If it means being different or being laughed at, I'm willing Lord. It doesn't matter that other people aren't doing it. If it takes more consecration, more time, more money, I'm willing to do it Lord because it needs to be done; and I'm not just going to look around to see what "Sister Jane" is doing on my left or "Brother Joe" is doing on my right. We'll do it together!"

Now, the first thing is self-denial and the second thing is separation. That's sanctification in the sense of separation. So let's say those two things: "Self-denial and Separation," if we're going to be used of God. Is this a missionary message? It is, very much so, because God is looking for people whom He can use in a special way.

SANCTIFICATION

All right, number three — no dead body. What would that mean? I think this is easier than the other two. Before you were saved, you were alive unto sin; and when you were saved, the old life died and you became a new creature in Christ Jesus. And now, the old ways are put aside and the old sins and habits of the past are put aside and we are to touch "no dead body." We are not to go back to the old way of living again. We live in a world where many professing Christians are compromising; living on the borderline and putting up with things which in "the old days" we didn't allow. Now, many of these are accepted. But, we sacrifice something when we don't hold the line of holiness. I say to you tonight — I believe that if we are going to be the people that God can use, we're going to have to get back to the place where we walk in holiness. Our speech must be holy. Our lives must be holy. Dirty jokes and shady behavior have to go if we're going to be what God wants us to be. Touch no dead body!

So, the three requirements of the man or women whom God is going to use here in Aurora who can rise above the norm of Christian behavior to the place where God can use them is the person who will deny themselves; who will be willing to be different — separate; and who will live a sanctified life. Let's say those three things together: "Self-denial, Separation, Sanctification!!"

Now, I'm going to tell you a story and it's going to be one of those "I'm going to begin to conclude" stories. It's going to take me a little while to conclude because I'm going to tell you the story about a Nazarite. A Nazarite who began right, then didn't go right, and then he ended up right. Hold onto those Faith Promise cards because after we look at the story, we're going to think about whether or not we're going to be the one that God is going to use in a special way. It is going to be a consecration service; a dedication service. We're going to talk about money, of course, about our commitment for this year, but we're also going to talk about dedicating ourselves for service. I hope there are people who will say, "Lord, here am I. Send me."

Morris and Macey served in Malawi and in South Africa before he was appointed as Field Director for the continent of Africa. They devoted 39 years to African work.

Okay, let's talk about this Nazarite named Samson. Before he was born, his mother and dad were visited by an angel. The angel said, "You're going to have a son, and your son is going to be a Nazarite! He's not to touch any wine; he's not to touch any dead body; he's not going to cut his hair! I'm going to use him to deliver My people from the Philistines." Oh, that was great news for Manoah and his wife! When the baby came, right from the beginning, they remembered God's promise and they raised the child accordingly. They never put a scissor to his hair and he grew up.

Now is the time for your imagination, because it doesn't say anything about from the time he was born to when he grew up. So, we have to fill in the gaps, and as we do, we'll do it in the context of this present day.

For Samson, it wouldn't be so bad up until the time he went to school. (Asking a boy in the audience) How old are you? You're eight? Okay, let's suppose that you had never cut your hair. It came time to go to school and your hair was way down like this, and all the other kids had short hair. Do you think it would have been easy? Would you have liked to have gone to school with long hair like that and have the kids laugh at you? Can you imagine the trauma? The kid would come home and say, "Mom, why do we have to be different? Why do I have to be different? Why can't I be like other kids?" Does that have a familiar ring, parents?

Then, I suppose Mrs. Manoah would take the little guy in her lap and say, "Now, listen. You don't understand, but before you were born, an angel spoke to me and said that God wants to use you to deliver our people." Does that make sense to an eight-year-old? No, it doesn't make any sense at all and a lot of times, parents, we impose our convictions on our kids. We don't understand why they don't accept it because we heard the voice of God, but they didn't. Then, let me say to the young people — evidently Samson had enough faith in his mom and dad to go along with what they said, whether he understood or not. I would encourage; even if you don't understand why mom and dad hold to certain rules, love them enough and trust them enough to obey, whether you understand or not.

Okay, so Samson's growing up now. He gets to be about 14 years old. School is torment — he hates it. He sneaks into school, waits for the bell to ring, sneaks into the back ally. Never goes to school through the front door. Gets into his seat and sits there, enduring it all and then when school is over, out he goes quickly before anybody can grab him and goes home again. It's intolerable! Once in awhile, the guys grab him, yank his hair and laugh at him. It's an awful life for a kid. Then, one day when he's about 14 (you won't find this in your Bible), he's going home and a couple of the guys grab him and begin to torment him and pull his hair. He's a normal kid, of course, and all of a sudden he loses his cool, and before he knows what he's doing, he takes his tormentors by the head and boom, boom!! Those kids go away saying, "Wow, that kid's strong. Wow!" And, Samson says, "Hey, that wasn't hard at all. That was easy. I think I'll do that tomorrow." So, the next day, instead of going down the back ally, he walks down the middle of the road, hoping. Sure enough, a couple of kids who hadn't seen him the day before and hadn't heard the news torment him. He grabs them gleefully and booms their heads together! The word spreads — "Leave Samson alone. He's strong!" Suddenly, Samson's chin comes up and he's glad he's a Nazarite. Everything his parents have been saying comes into focus and makes sense now.

Isn't it a wonderful day when our kids kneel at an altar and touch God for themselves?! They feel the power of God in their own lives then lift up their head and walk back into school saying, "I'm following Jesus. I love Him. He's my Lord." Because they themselves — not because of mom and dad or the church, but because they themselves touch God. Oh, I pray that tonight God will talk to our young people, that they will hear the voice of God until they'll want to commit themselves and be a deliverer for Jesus' sake and say, "Lord, here am I. Send me."

Now, we're getting back to the scriptures. It's getting that time now. He's getting bigger. How old does a young man have to be before he begins to look at girls? Well, he's getting at that age, and of course, Momma Manoah has already begun to pray that Samson will find a good girl to be his wife.

I remember when our girl got to the "old age" of 23 years and my wife had been praying. She got really desperate because she was so "old!" She began to pray that Virginia would find a husband and then when she found the fellow, she was afraid that she had the wrong one! See, you can't please somebody all the time.

Anyway, I'm sure Momma had been praying like this, and one day Samson came home and said, "Mom, I found her." And, Momma Manoah felt so good about it. She said, "Son, isn't that wonderful. Is she from Aurora First?" Samson sorta says, "Uh, no." "Oh, she's from one of the other churches in Denver?" "No." A little cold chill goes down the spine of Momma. A little apprehensive now, she says a little haltingly, "She is...a Christian isn't she?" "No." "Oh, who is she, Samson?" "She's a Philistine!" Can you imagine the trauma? These parents committed this child from birth to serving God, had heard the voice of God that this child was going to be used of God, and now, at this point of choosing a companion in life, he's going to blow the whole thing. Isn't it amazing that before this wonderful age when we begin to think of marriage, it's so easy to get down and say, "Lord, I'll go where you want me to go. I'll do what you want me to do." Then, suddenly, when we get to that age and look for a companion, we forget our commitment and our vows and say with Samson, "Get her for me. I want her." Now, I can imagine the home, the tears, the pleading, all was to no avail as this young man said, "No, sir. This is the girl I want and bless my soul, I'm going to have her. Get her for me." Well, I tell you the final straw was when Momma M said, "Well Samson, where does she live?" Then the roof fell in, 'cause he said, "She comes from Timnah!" "Do you know what you're saying? Timnah is the place of vineyards, the place where they have the grapes. What have you been doing in Timnah?"

I know what he'd been doing. He had been pleasing himself. He had laid aside his vow and was pleasing himself. Did God remove his power because he had broken his vow? No, God still used him, and he was able to accomplish a number of great feats. Samson did what so many of us do when God still blesses us in spite of our compromise. We say, "Well, praise the Lord, I can shout like I use to, I can preach, wasn't that a wonderful testimony? I felt the power of God, God can't feel too bad."

Don't fool yourself. This is the longsuffering of God Who is wanting, oh so much, to find people whom He can use; who will make the commitment over and above others. Samson thought he was getting by so he made a habit of going back down to Timnah to visit this girl; satisfying the flesh, doing anything he wanted to. And one day as he's going down to Timnah, a lion roars against him. He feels the power of God upon him and grabs that lion like it had been a kid and tears it apart and throws it aside and says, "Hallelujah! I'm full of the power of God. God still blesses me!"

Then, a few days later, walking down there as he goes along the path to Timnah, he remembers the lion and says, "Hum, I think I'll go check the lion." I'm sure the Spirit of God must have spoken to him and said, "Samson, touch no dead body." And he did what a lot of us do, he rationalizes, "I know what I'll do. I'll just go and look. I won't touch." I'll go down with the boys I use to drink with. I won't drink with them, I'll just visit with them. Maybe I can leave a witness. I'll just date that girl that's not a Christian. I won't touch her. I know I shouldn't. I won't touch her; I'll just date her.

So, he went to where the carcass was even though the command was clear. A Nazarite was not to touch a dead body. Rationalizing again, he approaches this carcass recalling the pleasure that day when God used him. All of a sudden he hears a little sound. Buzz — buzz. His eyes open wide. Honey! Honey in the carcass. Something sweet in sin; hadn't expected this. You said you were just going to look and not touch, but you didn't realize how clever the devil is. He always puts honey in the carcass!

Now Samson had a problem: how do you get honey out of a carcass without touching the carcass? How do you get the sweetness out of sin without sinning? He's circling the lion's carcass, going to reach in; didn't want to touch it but he wanted the honey, and one thing he hadn't anticipated — the passions of his body. His mouth begins to water; he's consumed with the desire for the honey. Hungry, he's gotten himself into a situation now where he can't back out. He's trying to maintain a right position as far as the Nazarite vow is concerned, but the desire overwhelms him so greatly that suddenly he throws caution to the wind, plunges his hand down and takes the honey to eat it. After he's done and has satisfied his passion, he realizes he's broken the third part of his vow. Oh, how often have Christians whom

God has used compromised, returned to sinful living and then rationalized their behavior. Oh they're Christians alright, part of the group. They still go through the motions, but like Samson, they explain away their behavior.

Obviously, Samson thinks to himself, "God, even if I cut my hair, it wouldn't make any difference. I can still preach; it doesn't really matter." So, the day he laid his head on Delilah's lap and told her everything about his power, he never for one moment thought he'd lose it. He had flaunted God's authority by not denying himself, by touching the dead carcass; and he fooled himself into thinking he could just go right on doing what he was doing. You know what happened. Delilah says, "Samson, the Philistines are here." He jumps up saying, "I'll do it like I did before." But, the power had gone and he was reduced to being just like any other Israelite. God couldn't use him. They put his eyes out and threw him into prison. I'm so glad it doesn't end here. . .

There's hope tonight, I want you to know that. Take hold of those Faith Promise cards. Think of the ministry God wants for you, the way God wants to use you; what you can accomplish for God at Aurora First Assembly. Think of Samson.

They put him in prison and I think out of the holes where his eyes had been, the tears flowed down his cheeks. Samson prayed, "God, give me one more chance. One more opportunity to be the man you can use." As he prayed, his hair grew longer, and then one day the little boy came and led him out to the arena. They wanted to laugh at him, but I'm sure as the kid took him by the arm, a tingle went through his body. Samson thought, "Is this the time when God is going to use me again?" They took him to the temple of Dagon and the crowd began to laugh. He said, "I don't care, God, let them laugh. Just this one time God, let me be used for Your glory. Let me be the man You can use again. Even if I die, it doesn't matter. I'll deny myself. Let me do Your will, Lord."

As he was led to the supporting columns in the arena, he prayerfully bent into the pillar and suddenly felt the power of God again. The strength surged and as he pulled the pillars together, the temple came tumbling down. Samson did a greater work in his death than he had done in his life!

Now, bow your heads in prayer. Here at Aurora First, we have a chance to be a church that is not the ordinary church. A church that can rise above the normal; a missionary church! A church that goes to the ends of the earth with the Gospel of Jesus Christ. Some of you young people can surrender your desires to God tonight, and He will lay His hand upon you and set you apart. You can say, "I'll follow Jesus. I'll be what God wants me to be." Businessman, God can take your business, and you can rise above the ordinary to where that business will be used by God.

It's not too late. Maybe you drifted from God's best plan for your life. You haven't denied yourself. Selfishness may have crept in. But tonight, God's talking to you and He says, "I'm going to give you another chance. I'm giving you an opportunity to be used!"

Del and Marlys Kingsriter, as they headed for East Africa in 1954, with David, Joan, and Bryan.

REV. DELMAR KINGSRITER

Those who have never experienced it cannot fully comprehend the force of the Divine Call upon a career missionary. Del Kingsriter demonstrates so vividly what this generation of Christians refers to as "purpose."

When he and Marlys sensed the missionary call, they were first turned down in 1953 by the foreign missions director of the denomination. A year later, they were again rebuffed — not for lack of qualifications, but because the missions department lacked funds, being actually $100,000 in the red! However, Del was so convinced of the call and since they were short of funds themselves (raising a family and pastoring a small church), he hitchhiked from Northern Minnesota to the church headquarters in Springfield, Missouri! The last guy to give him a ride was going the opposite direction, but something prompted him to turn around and ask the transient preacher where he was going? The man delivered Del to the front door of the Assemblies of God and the determined missionary walked into the office of the director — Rev. Noel Perkin — thirty minutes before Perkin was to leave on a trip!

When Mr. Perkin saw Del's determination, he granted appointment on the spot with, of course, no financial guarantees! He and Marlys served from that moment in June of 1954 until the day of Del's death, April 26, 1997. Their ministry took them to Tanganyika (now Tanzania), Malawi, and Kenya. They then served the Center for Ministry to Muslims for 13 years.

Del was a "man's man" — a big game hunter and photographer whose movie on East African wild game achieved national prominence on U.S. network television. His friends knew him as absolutely fearless, whether facing down a water buffalo, a lion or a Mau Mau guerilla.

Del Kingsriter was a personal friend. Margie and I spent many hours of enjoyable fellowship with Del and Marlys, his talented and lovely wife, including a photo safari across the Serengeti Game Preserve in Kenya. In 1980, Del was my host when preaching the Kenya General Council in Kisumu, on the shores of Lake Victoria. Del prompted us to raise a considerable amount of funds for the East African School of Theology, one of his many projects. Del fought cancer for over 17 years and it never stopped him until just a few days before his death. He preached the following message in 1984, on one of his many trips to Aurora.

— H. C.

8

"THE PRIMARY GOAL OF THE CHURCH"

Rev. Delmar Kingsriter

Do you know what the true goal, the true purpose for this church is? If I were to ask you tonight to write out your answer on a piece of paper, I'm sure I'd have many answers.

Today there are people who are saying that the true purpose of the church is to stand up and be counted; to be a voice against social evils. After reading your newspapers yesterday, I think you ought to stand up and shout it out in a declaration against some of the evils in your own city.

Some would say that the church should be a vehicle to help people who are in need and we certainly agree. I come from an area where there is great human suffering. Ethiopia alone last year had 250,000 people die of starvation. I can't even comprehend that myself, although I've been there and seen some of it. There is so much poverty and suffering; we do have an obligation. I thank you for helping. Last year, through my office, we were able to distribute over $50,000 worth of foodstuffs to hungry Africans.

But, the true goal of the church, friends, is set by Jesus Christ Himself in Mark's Gospel the 16th chapter when He said, "Go ye into all the world and preach the gospel to every creature." That is the goal which we must always keep before us. It is primary!! And, I thank God that when I come to this church, I see that you are on course. God bless you. That is your primary goal in this church; I can see it; I can feel it in the air. I want to thank you for that and the leaders of this church for having this as their purpose.

So tonight — you know sometimes it's important that you measure your progress against your goal. Corporations all set goals and then, periodically, they have stockholder's meetings. So, you are sort of like stockholders and I'm going to give you a report on Eastern Africa. I want to give you some good news.

As you look back through the pages of history, you'll find that the Church, in many cases, grew weak and failed in fulfilling the Great Commission. But, in my opinion, there has never been a day since that job description was given to the Church when the Church has taken more seriously that Commission. And, I would venture to say, that there has never been a day when more people, and this includes apostolic days, when more people have been swept into the Kingdom of God than have been added in this past year!

When I was in Ethiopia in May of this year, staying in a little hotel room (I don't think the automobile club rated it!); a little 8 × 10 room with a 2 × 2 window in one corner, letting in a little light — just big enough to put a single bed, a table, and a chair, it was enough to depress anyone! I awakened the next morning and I felt depressed. The circumstances; the surroundings may have had something to do with it, but I don't think so. I have been to Ethiopia many times since we had to evacuate our missionaries. We didn't evacuate because they were in danger of their lives. I don't think a missionary should ever evacuate because of danger. I don't read in the Bible where people were called upon to pray to spare us from danger; God help us if that is our philosophy! We left the country because we were a danger to the Christians who were there. Whenever they were seen with us, they were arrested.

This Marxist regime is determined to stamp out the Church, and our church there, a virile, vibrant church of 25,000 members, was the first church in Ethiopia banned because it was appealing to the youth! The revival especially reached university students. I've been back to that church to visit many times and never once have been permitted to preach. Not once could I pass out literature on the streets. I was discouraged about that. I had just returned from Somalia and saw such darkness, and I said, "God, how are we going to do it? How can we reach the world if we can't preach?"

You see, one of the thrilling things about this day is if you can ever get a preacher, you are going to have a church! It is just as simple as that because, friends, God is moving in this world. Dr. Barrett, who did a phenomenal work of study on church growth, stated in his book that the most powerful force in the world of missions today is the Charismatic force. God is moving by His Spirit in the world today.

But, that day in Ethiopia, I was despondent and discouraged. Have any of you gotten that way? Do you think that missionaries sometimes have downers? We do, and I said, "God you've got to help me today. You have to give me a word." I opened my Bible and did something I don't really advise you to do, but you know, sometimes you get kind of desperate and a little foolish! I said, "Lord, I'm going to open this Bible, and wherever it opens, that will be the "word" for me today." The Bible fell open to Psalm 46, and as I read it, I came to that part where it says, "Be still and know that I am God. I will be exalted among the nations!" Oh, hallelujah! I felt like I could run through a troop and leap over a wall! God had said something to me. He also gave me Psalm 67, verse 2 — "That Thy saving health shall be among the nations," and then, the last verse, "God shall bless thee and all the ends of the earth shall fear Him!" Praise God!

I have news for you; all these self-styled empire builders and dictators of the world, the Bible says one day are going to bow their knee before the King of Kings and Lord of Lords and confess Him as the real King! Oh, that thrills me!

So, as I read those portions of the Psalms, it so encouraged me. I went out and had lunch with a young man who is one of our pastors in Ethiopia and said to him, "How is it going?" This is a "Smyrna Church!" That is, if a person has a job and it becomes known that he is a Christian, he will lose his job. It is exactly what it was in the days of the Smyrna church of Revelation. The church is going through great persecution. This pastor had just come out of prison, having spent seven months and twenty days. The only crime he committed was that he was caught witnessing and trying to encourage one of his Christian brothers. When I asked him how it was going I said, "Is there fragmentation in the church? Are people drifting away because of this persecution?" He looked me in the eye with a smile and said, "Oh no, Brother Kingsriter. There's a deepening in the faith, and we are seeing great growth in the church! University students are coming to our secret cell meetings and are finding Christ."

The next day, I had an interview with another leader and said to him, "How is it going in your area?" "Oh," he said, "it's tremendous! There are many trials. Several of our pastors have been killed because of their witness for Jesus. But, Communism is no match for Christ!" Hallelujah! That's good news, isn't it!

I spoke with Jerry Spain and he told me how a man walked onto the campus of E.A.S.T. (East African School of Theology in Nairobi), dressed in his Kioski. He wore the tassels and garb of the Coptic Church of Ethiopia. That's the state church; it was the state church before the Marxist revolution. It is such a powerful group the revolutionary leaders have not had the nerve to touch it. They've been able to continue their work, although it is questionable how effective they are since they have very little semblance of an evangelical witness. But, this priest came to our campus with a letter in his hand from the head of the Coptic Church. It said something like, "This young man has been given a scholarship to go to England to study in a theological seminary. But, we've heard there is a Charismatic school in Nairobi and we are sending him to you. We would like him to attend your school because we want him to come back to our country with the secret of your life!"

Jerry said, "What shall we do?" I said, "Take him!"

We usually have a screening and require all sorts of references, but I said to take him. So, he filled out an application form, and

Margie Cummings, Marlys and Del Kingsriter during a visit to East Africa in 1980.

then disappeared. Some time later, I received a call from Jerry, who said, "Guess who's here?" He told me that the Coptic priest had now come to enroll in our school! Wow! Can you imagine what that might do in Ethiopia when he returns with the power and life of the Holy Spirit? I tell you, God knows how to do it! God knows how to put things together. And friend, let me tell you something; it's not just happening overseas. Your life may be fragmented and you may be drifting. I followed a car the other day with a bumper sticker that read, "I'm drifting!" I thought, "Oh, how true; how true!" So many people with no meaning in life. But, if you'll just put yourself at God's disposal, He can put you together and give you purpose!!

In Luke chapter 5, there's a story similar to mine. It's of the all-night fishing trip that saw no results. You hear Simon Peter saying, "Master, we have toiled all night and have taken nothing. Nevertheless, at Thy Word, I will let down the net."

This centers around the calling of the first disciples and it has special significance for us today, for Jesus, when He had finished with the miracle, turned to His Disciples and said, "Ye shall be fishers of men." You remember the story. The Disciples were professional fishermen and they had gone out as usual, fishing all night. They knew where the best fishing holes were and had covered every place in the lake, working themselves to exhaustion, and caught absolutely nothing. Now, as they're sitting there discouraged, along comes a Carpenter who knows nothing about fishing and says, "Let's go fishing!"

I can hear them saying to themselves, "You know, there's something wrong here." But, they didn't say much, except for Peter. He was always the spokesman. He said, "Well, Lord, you know we've been out working and we're supposed to know everything about fishing, and to be honest, it's not very good right now. Night time is bad enough, but fishing in the day is worse."

But Simon Peter inserted one word — nevertheless. "In the natural it seems impossible and it may seem foolish, but because You asked me to, I'm going to."

Once I was driving in Tanzania to visit our missionaries to determine what their cost of living was so that we could adjust their budgets; they didn't feel that the cost of living index the department had was adequate. The cost of living in Tanzania had skyrocketed because of the volatile economy. As I neared the city of Arusha, I passed the Baptist Seminary and thought of my friend, Dr. Tom McMillan, a Southern Baptist doctor who could have returned home to America at any time and drawn any kind of salary he would name. Many people would say that he has thrown away 25 years of his life there in that little village; a place where you couldn't even buy flour or sugar. I had taken a list of the ten commodities we would consider essential to life and had asked our missionaries to give me the price of each; a pound of butter, a pound of flour, and so forth. They replied that five of the ten were not even available, and that butter was $11 per pound! I asked myself this question as I passed the seminary: "Why would Tom McMillan do it? Why would he do what others would consider to be wasting his life?"

Someone once asked David Livingstone that question: "Why would you give your whole life to Africa?" It was well known that Livingstone could have enjoyed a life of luxury. He was now famous. He replied, "If it be considered an honor to obey a commission by an earthly king, can it be a sacrifice to obey the Commission of the King of Kings?"

There is only one reason Tom McMillan would do what he does and why other missionaries do what they do — it's because Jesus told them to do it. It's just as simple as that. Obedience is rated very high on God's priorities, friends. I've told my wife many times, "Honey, I wouldn't do this for all the money in the world; I will only do it for Jesus!"

Let me take you back a little in the "history of missionary fishing." For years, many of our missionaries worked a term, some of them a lifetime, with very little result. Warren Muldricker, a missionary with the Sudan Interior Mission, spent 13 years in Somalia before the government asked them to leave. I recently saw Warren, now 70 years of age, and I said, "Warren, if there should be a change in government and they would allow you to go back, would you

Mr. Kingsriter stands with the "finished product" of a missionary career — a new generation of trained Christian leaders at the East African School of Theology. Del served in Tanganyika, Malawi, and Kenya for 30 years. The concluding 13 years of his life were spent with the Center for Ministry to Muslims.

do it?" He replied, "In a minute!" He worked 13 years and was not able to establish one church. How would you like to do that? I think I would get discouraged and say, "I'll wipe the dust off my feet!" Thirteen years!

The history of missions is replete with examples exactly like Warren Muldricker. Men who gave their lives. I quote from H. B. Garlock's book, ***"Before We Kill and Eat You!"*** when he said of Liberia, that the death rate was so high that many mission societies decided to pull out. Of 79 missionaries sent out by the CMS of London, 44 died in the first year! Of 75 sent by the Presbyterian Church USA, 35 died and many who survived were sent home, broken in health. Many lost what was dearest to them — their children. But, they pressed on. Many of them mastered difficult languages, committed unwritten languages to written, and for years labored without any fruit. It's been a long, lonely night for many of our missionaries in Africa, Asia, and other areas of the world.

Missions researchers in California fed church growth statistics for many years into a computer and made a startling discovery; suddenly they saw that they could pinpoint, almost to the year, when there was a phenomenal growth of the Church on mission fields. I can testify to this personally. For 18 years I labored, walking from village to village, traveling by dug out canoes, pedaling bicycles, every means of transportation, trying to get to where the people needed the Gospel. We saw some results; but then 12 years ago something began to happen! I can't explain it. I'm still the same man. I still preach the same message. I think I prayed as much when I was a young missionary as I do now, but we are seeing a growth in the Church that is phenomenal!

Let me offer one illustration: At the World Pentecostal Conference in 1982, a man came up to me. His name was Blackburn and he said, "I am with our fellowship in Mauritius." (How many have heard of Mauritius? How many know what a Dodo bird is? This is where it came from; now extinct.) He told me how a French evangelist had come there years before. He held a little crusade and this guy, Blackburn, was saved and began to preach. He still works fulltime with the Mauritius government as a social worker. Every night of the week, he and his wife are out preaching on the street corners and in the churches they have established. He said, "I would like for you to come and see what God has done."

I said, "Sure, we'll come." So, we set a time, and when I arrived at the airport and we were driving away, he said, "Brother Kingsriter, you are going to be famous on this island." It's only a small island with barely a million people, so I said, "What do you mean?"

He pointed to a tree and said, "Look over there." On every post and tree and little building, there was a great big poster with my picture on it. "Del Kingsriter, Evangelist, will preach in the crusade."

Now, I'm not a crusade preacher and I had Dr. George Flattery with me, so I said, "George, you're going to do the preaching!" He said, "Oh no, I'm not. You're the guy on the poster!"

I don't know how Blackburn had gotten my picture; I still don't know! They had my passport photo. They said that if you look anything like your passport picture, you're too sick to travel! But, he had taken it, blown it up as big as he could!

Mauritius is an island which is 57% Asian and the balance is native tribes. I will never forget standing in that civic auditorium. We arrived early and every seat was already filled and they were carrying in benches on their heads and chairs for people to sit. They don't have fire marshals so they filled the aisles. They had one of those old theater stages — a great big one — and you could stand up there and look down at the crowd. I was scared! People standing inside and out, listening to me over the loud speakers! As I began to preach, I felt the Spirit of God come upon me, and when I gave the altar call, I was not prepared for what I saw! Islamic peoples, Mauritian tribesmen, people of Chinese descent, streaming down the aisles, elbowing their way, trying to get through to Jesus! It was so exciting! It wasn't me. It's the Holy Spirit who is moving in the world and here were people, bound in their Islamic tradition being saved!!

How many believe God is able to accomplish His task of building His Church? Consider what happened that day when the disciples went out in the boat at Jesus' command. I believe Jesus talked to the fish! Do you think fish can understand Jesus? There are many places in Scripture where God talked to fish and they heard Him.

I think Jesus said to the fish, "Come on over." And, I can see the fish coming from every part of that lake; swimming as fast as they could swim! Some of them jumping out of the water, trying to get into that net. Some of them may have even jumped into the boat!

You don't think that is possible? Someone has said regarding the raising of Lazarus that when Jesus said, "Lazarus, come forth," it was good that He said "Lazarus" instead of simply saying "Come forth!" If He hadn't identified Lazarus as the one He wanted to come out of that grave, all of the graves in Bethany and Jerusalem would have opened, because of the power of our Lord!

Friends, I believe with all my heart that, when God speaks, something is going to happen! Jesus just said to those fish, "come," and they came and filled the nets so much that Simon Peter said, "Help! I've got too many fish. I don't know what to do with all of them! Send some more boats!"

As I see what is happening in the world today, it has to be that God is moving by His Spirit. In the natural, when we see the job — the unfinished task — we declare that it can't be done. I think Ezekiel must have felt like that when God told him to prophesy to those dead bones, but by faith he was obedient and he did what God told him to do, and the Bible says that God raised up a great army and the whole valley was full of live people!

I don't know how God is going to put it all together; but I know one thing, that as God's prophets, you and I, are going forth on the face of this earth, God is bringing together a mighty army. The nets are getting filled.

But, one of our greatest challenges: spiritual awakenings can be preserved only if people are stabilized and taught the Word of God. The bottom line of missions is the training of nationals who will, in turn, blaze new trails. Then, they can nurture and train these people, grounding them in the Word of God. In this, the establishment of Bible Colleges and training centers; we need your help. As your pastor felt the burden for the East Africa School of Theology, so the need is for others to pick up the responsibility.

We haven't yet been permitted into countries such as Sudan, but we can get students out who will travel to one of our Bible Colleges. Through this procedure, we are actually getting into Sudan, Somalia, Ethiopia, and other so-called "closed countries."

Can you begin to see how excited I become when I share what God is doing. This is what Pastor Cummings felt when he came to Kenya and told us you wanted a part in this ministry through your "Together We Build" program.

This great enterprise was founded in sacrifice by our Lord and Savior Jesus Christ. Your pastor tells me that this church last year gave $200,000 to missions in the teeth of recession. I know your building programs are going on, and I congratulate you friends because you have continued to sacrifice for missions. I once heard a pastor say, "Don't tell me it doesn't hurt when you give to missions. If it doesn't hurt, you're not giving enough!" But, if we do our best for Jesus, we're going to have a part in what's going to happen. As your pastor reminded us today, we've read the last chapter and God's going to be victorious! The only question is, "Am I going to be a part of it?"

REV. HAROLD CARLBLOM

Before his homegoing, Margie and I knew Harold and Jean Carlblom for over three decades of ministry. As missionaries to Indonesia, they ministered in each of the three churches we pastored. Their passion for the lost in the world's largest Islamic nation was legendary.

The Carlbloms first went to Indonesia in 1946, just as the Pacific theater of World War II military action was wrapping up. These pioneer missionaries to that region left an indelible imprint on the nation and the national leaders. After graduating from one of the first classes of ministerial students at North Central Bible Institute (now North Central University) in Minneapolis, the Carlbloms were married in 1935. Plunging energetically into gospel ministry, they pastored churches in Burwell, Nebraska; Detroit, Michigan; Kalispell, Montana; and Tacoma, Washington. Their next move was a natural — across the wide Pacific to Indonesia. Harold and Jean Carlblom served the nation and people they loved until 1985.

Harold Carlblom preached this message in our Aurora Missions Crusade on November 14, 1982. His impassioned appeal so moved a dear elderly, retired gentleman in our congregation that he wrote out a check for the total cost of constructing a church building in Indonesia. One of many buildings the Carlbloms sponsored, it stands as a tribute to the man who challenged American Christians to "Slack Not!"

— H. C.

Harold and Jean Carlblom and three daughters, as they arrived in Indonesia in 1946. They would serve in this largest of the Muslim nations until 1985.

9

"SLACK NOT!"

Rev. Harold Carlblom

We have known your pastors for many years, having had the joy of ministering in their churches in Wyoming, South Dakota, and now in Colorado. I can say that in nearly 37 years of missions, I have never found a pastor as missionary minded as your pastor. He has already told you we are missionaries to Indonesia, the fifth most populous nation in the world and the largest Muslim nation. Indonesia is a nation of islands which include Borneo, Sumatra, and part of New Guinea. Lest you should think that I normally wear such loud clothes to church, this is my Indonesian costume. The hat is worn by Indonesian men. The jacket is made of Batik cloth. Very sincerely I say that if I had more time to give for Jesus, I'd do it in Indonesia. We love the people and we love our work.

From the book of Joshua, chapter 10, I read the sixth verse: "And the men of Gibeon sent unto Joshua to the camp at Gilgal saying, '**Slack not** thy hand from thy servants. Come up to us quickly and save us and help us, for all the kings of the Amorites that dwell in the mountains are gathered together against us.' So Joshua ascended from Gilgal. He and all the people of war with him and all the mighty men of valour. And the Lord said unto Joshua, 'Fear them not, for I have delivered them into thine hand. There shall not a man of them stand before thee.' Joshua therefore came unto them suddenly and went up from Gilgal all night."

This was the occasion when the Gibeonites surrendered their royal city to Joshua and the invading Israelites because of fear. They had seen the conquest of Jericho and what had happened to Ai, so they made a deal with Joshua in return for protection. Then, there were five kings of the Amorites who formed an alliance and agreed that they would smite Gibeon for making peace with Israel. Paul later writes to the Corinthians that the things which happened in the Old Testament were physical examples of things that happen in the spiritual realm. Accordingly, as we see these five pagan kings coming up against Gibeon because of their coalition with Joshua, it represents the forces of Satan. Satanic forces around the world are seeking to enslave the peoples of this world. Joshua represents the Lord Jesus, and the forces that were with him would represent the Church of the Living God.

The lesson is clear; that we might come to help those who are in desperate straights. Satan's plan from the beginning has been to destroy those whom God had created for His glory. Early in the civilization of the world, sin became so prevalent that God purposed to destroy the world because of the influence of the enemy. Down through time we see a great effort on the part of Satan to destroy the works of God, when on the Cross of Calvary he thought he had gained the victory over the Son of God — sent to be the Savior of the world. As we study further in the Word of God, we're told how in the end time, the forces of Satan will gather all the armies of the world to destroy the works of God and fight against the Lord.

So, today in this great Missions Crusade, we are aware of the fact that as we set our goals on winning the world for Christ, we have an enemy who is out there, seeking to destroy; seeking to hinder in every way, and as the people of Gibeon cried out, others cry out to us — "Don't slack now! — Come up and help us and save us!" The Gibeonites realized they were facing annihilation.

You know, friends, God's love has been displayed toward the whole world. From both the Old and New Testaments, we see it. Through Ezekiel, God said, "Turn ye, turn ye, for why will ye die?" Then, to prove His love, He gave His only begotten Son "that whosoever believeth in Him should not perish but have everlasting life."

God is concerned about "Gibeonites!" He's concerned about the people of the great nation of China. He's concerned about the people in the islands of Indonesia. He wants to save them; He doesn't want them to perish. He doesn't want Satan to have an advantage over them and take them so He's calling upon each of us as His rescue force, that we may rally and hear their cry. That every one of us do what we can.

Young people — you who are of the younger generation, you can look at my gray hair and realize that Jean and I do not have very long to continue laboring for God. But, friends, there is such an urgency of the hour; such a need at this present time that I pray God may stir you to the depths of your being to give yourself completely to Him!

Out in Indonesia, we came to a little city in East Java; the children of an elderly man were members of our church there. But, the father had never given his heart to Christ. We were put up in the home of these Indonesian people and when this happens, we generally spend our time in the home eating meals with them and identifying with them. This old man came to our services. It was the first time he had ever been to the church, although it was a stone's throw from his house. He was a Muslim. A few days later, as we were leaving that home after the meetings, tears were in his eyes as he said, "I have never given my heart to Christ before, but I have felt God's love as you have been in our home; you have shown us the love of Jesus! I have now given my heart to Christ." A smile came over his face as the tears rolled down his cheeks! Praise God!

It makes us think of the time of the Gibeonites. As those five kings were ready to wipe them out, their cry to Israel was "Slack not thy hand from thy servants. Come up to us quickly and save us and help us." Friends, there is such an urgency today. A world that is now approaching five billion* and the greater percentage of them have yet to hear the Name of Jesus. Nothing of this wonderful Gospel which has brought light and joy and blessing to our hearts. We must not just "play church" or "play at missions." We must really put our shoulders to the wheel. You and I need to do what we can.

I will never forget the joy we had when some of the people from the little church we started said, "Our grandmother has never heard about Jesus. Would you come and tell her?" So, we took our national pastor, because she spoke the Javanese dialect. We spoke to the grandmother through the Javanese pastor lady; the old woman was 101 years old! As I laid my hand on her shoulder and saw her wrinkled old face light up, suddenly a smile began to creep over that face as we told her that Jesus was ready to forgive her sins and take her to heaven. We said, "Hallelujah!" Friends you may not know what joy is. That is why Jean and I are not ready to quit yet; we feel we want to keep going as long as we can. There is such a reward, such joy and fulfillment in being a missionary. I want you to believe me; I'm not just up here speak-

*Editor's note: World population is now past six billion.

ing words, but I'm saying from my heart that there's a real reward for all of us committed to missions. There's a reward for you who support missions and make faith promises. I believe there will be the same reward for you as there is for us.

"Slack not they hand" was the message sent to Joshua. I want to say, friends, "let's not slack our hand when it comes to **prayer**!" The Lord Jesus told us to "Pray ye the Lord of the harvest that He will send forth laborers into the harvest field." We must pray to that end, because it takes the call of God to make a minister and send a laborer into the harvest field. We have seven Bible schools in Indonesia, training national young men and women for ministry; there are hundreds of students in classes today. And, it takes prayer to bring the true call of God to each of them if they are to become laborers.

Slack not thy hand in prayer. Once, when we were going upstream in Borneo, way into the interior by motorboat, we had to go through an area where the river narrowed and became very swift. There were whirlpools large enough in that river to take down many of the native canoes and even our small motorboat. So, I was quite concerned. I turned the controls over to one of the nationals who knew the river. Although we had the engine fully throttled to 1,800 revolutions per minute, the thing wide open, I looked at the trees on either side of the river and it looked like we were just standing still in the middle of that rushing water! I really wondered if we would make it. Would we be sucked into a whirlpool? Well, thank God, we got through and moved above the area where we could minister the Word of God. We're here to tell the story!!

Years later, we heard from a dear saint of God back in the States who said, "What happened at such and such a time on this date?

I had a burden for you and felt God moving me to pray!" Friends that time corresponded with the very moment we were in those dangerous waters!! God had moved upon this lady to slack not her hand! So, let it prompt each one to respond when it comes to praying for your missionaries! Slack not thy hand in prayer!!

In the book of First Timothy, Paul said, "Therefore I exhort that, first of all, supplications, prayers, intercessions, and giving of thanks be made for all men. For this is good and acceptable in the sight of God our Savior, who will have all men to be saved and come to the knowledge of the truth." God wants the world to be saved. You say, "Well, that's an impossibility now. The coming of the Lord is near."

Well, friends, I believe in miracles. As we return to our text, remember that Joshua was fighting against five kings of the Amorites. It tells us in verses 12 and 13 of that chapter, when the day was beginning to end, the sun was going down, Joshua, the man of God with the authority that God had given him, said, "Sun, stand thou still upon Gibeon; and thou, Moon, in the valley of Ajalon. The sun stood still, and the moon stayed, until the people had avenged themselves upon their enemies."

Friends, you and I have access to the throne of God! Jesus said that if we have faith, we can move mountains. Hallelujah! We can stop the sun! We can cause the moon to stand still. And, I believe that, through prayer, God can help us see miracles accomplished! Amen. Let's not have a "small" God, but let's believe in the greatness of our God and "slack not our hand" when it comes to praying on behalf of the needy souls around the world.

"Slack not thy hand" when it comes to being **ready to act!** God wants minutemen — people who are ready at the drop of the hat to give themselves wholly to His work and to whatever He may call them to do. Young man, young woman, there is work for you to do, and I pray that you will not waste your life in trivial matters or things of this world. I gave my heart to Jesus when I was 17 and I thank the Lord, because He has enabled me to spend 52 years for Him. Glory to God! And, I thank the Lord that you too may have this opportunity. Your pastor mentioned on the night of the banquet of Esther when she was in Persia and Mordecai, who said, "Who knows but what you are come to the kingdom for such a time as this!!" She was ready to act, and when she saw the tremendous need, she said, "You pray and we will pray and then I will go to see the king, and if I perish, I perish!" She was ready to lay down her life upon the altar of commitment for her people. You know, friends, this is the thing that God is counting on from His people today, and I pray that God will speak to us all to be ready to act.

Rev. Harold Carlblom effectively and passionately presented the cause of missions amongst the people he loved for almost 40 years.

"Slack not thy hand" when it comes to **sacrifice.** I read in the Gospel of Luke chapter 9 that, "when the time was come for Jesus to be received up, He steadfastly set His face to go to Jerusalem." It took a steadfast setting of His face to not turn aside. In the garden, He prayed "If it be Your will, let this cup pass from Me, but, not My will but Thine be done!" You know, friends, God wants us that we may make a consecration to where we are ready to sacrifice for Jesus. A dear little old Swedish lady in Minneapolis, Mother Swanson, where we started our ministry years ago is an example. We were itinerating to go out the first time, and this dear little lady was in the service on a Sunday morning. I preached on enlargement of the heart and Mother Swanson was weeping when she came to greet me at the close of the service. She said, "God has spoken to me, and I want you to come to my house tomorrow morning." So, we went to her home. She lived on the third story of an apartment, having rented out the two lower stories of her house to support herself. She was almost up in the attic, it seemed; real steep stairs going up. She was eighty years of age and, as Mother Swanson received us that morning, she began to weep again and said, "God spoke to me about making a sacrifice for you." So, she reached into her blouse and pulled out a $100 bill. I had rarely seen a $100 bill at that time! It was back in 1946. I just started praising God for it and I thanked her so much, but she reached in and got another one! And, another one! And, another one! She didn't stop until there were ten $100 bills!

Mother Swanson has since gone on to be with the Lord, but she said on that day that God had asked her to sacrifice. It may have been all of her savings, we don't know, but she did it because she wanted to help a young missionary couple get to the field of their calling. I'm not exaggerating when I say that we've seen literally thousands of people who have come to Christ as we have ministered in Good News Crusades and Mother Swanson is going to share in the reward. Hallelujah!! Oh, brothers and sisters, may the Lord stir all of our hearts that we may not slack our hand in sacrifice; to go and to give and to do what we can for Jesus.

One more thought — we don't want to "slack our heart" when it comes to **love.** As I was praying this morning in our hotel room, the Lord impressed me with the words of Moses when Moses was standing before the Lord because the children of Israel had sinned. He said, "Forgive them of their sins, but if not, blot my name out of the book which you have written." Love was so great in the heart of Moses that he was ready to have his own name removed from God's Book, if necessary, to save a stiff-necked, hard-hearted people. That's love!

The Apostle Paul is another good example when he said, "I have continual sorrow and heaviness of heart. I could wish myself accursed from Christ for my brethren, my kinsmen according to the flesh." Oh, my brothers and sisters, God wants us to love the world. God wants us to love souls.

The cry today is "slack not thine heart; slack not thine hand." Oh, may God stir our hearts to give our best.

Paul saw the Macedonian in a vision when the man said, "Come over to Macedonia and help us." People are crying like that in Indonesia! They are crying from China; they are crying from Palau; they are crying from all over the world! "Come and help us. Come and save us, before it is too late!"

God bless you!

They Still Speak Order Form

Use this convenient order form to order
They Still Speak

PLEASE PRINT:

Name: ______________________________

Address: ______________________________

City: ____________________ State: __________

Zip: ______________________________

Phone: (   ) ______________________________

________ copies of book @ $12.95 each $________

Postage and handling @ $1.50 per book $________

Total amount Enclosed $________

Make checks payable to First Ministries

PLEASE CHARGE MY: MUST BE COMPLETED IN FULL

☐ Visa ☐ MasterCard Amount $ ____________________

Name on card ______________________________

Card #
☐☐☐☐ ☐☐☐☐ ☐☐☐☐ ☐☐☐☐

Signature ____________________ Expiration date________

Phone #(______)______________________________

Send to:
First Ministries
P.O. Box 440267, Aurora, CO 80044-0267